T   TO THE BEST CANADIAN SKIING   E

C 1

796   The Insider's guide to the best Canadian skiing. -- 1st
.93   ed. (1992)-   . -- New York ; Toronto : Fodor's
02571   Travel, c1992-
Ins   v. : maps.

Spine title: Canadian skiing.
06583849   ISBN:0679024409 (pbk.)

1. Skis and skiing - Canada - Guidebooks. I. Title:
Canadian skiing.

THE INSIDER'S GUIDE

TO THE BEST CANADIAN SKIING

BY CLIVE HOBSON

Fodor's Travel Publications, Inc.
New York, London, Toronto,
Sydney, Auckland

Copyright © 1992 by Clive Hobson

Fodor's is a trademark of Fodor's Travel Publications, Inc.

All rights reserved under International and Pan-American Copyright Conventions. Published in the United States by Fodor's Travel Publications, Inc., a subsidiary of Random House, Inc., New York, and simultaneously in Canada by Random House of Canada Limited, Toronto. (Distributed by Random House, Inc., New York)

Canadian Cataloguing in Publication Data

Hobson, Clive

   The insider's guide to the best Canadian skiing

ISBN 0-679-02440-9

1. Skis and skiing – Canada – Guidebooks.

I. Title.

GV854.8.C3H62 1992   796.93'025'71   C92-094646-1

First Edition

The Insider's Guide to the Best Canadian Skiing

Text design and map illustrations: Teri McMahon

Jacket design: Fabrizio La Rocca, Tigist Getachew

Cover photo: Paul Morrison

Special Sales

Fodor's Travel Publications are available at special discounts for bulk purchases (100 copies or more) for sales promotions or premiums. Special editions, including personalized covers, excerpts of existing guides, and corporate imprints, can be created in large quantities for special needs. For more information write to Special Marketing, Fodor's Travel Publications, 201 East 50th St., New York, NY 10022. Inquiries from the United Kingdom should be sent to Fodor's Travel Publications, 20 Vauxhall Bridge Rd., London, England SW1V 2SA. Inquiries from Canada should be sent to Marketing Department, Random House of Canada Ltd., 1265 Aerowood Drive, Mississauga, Ontario, L4W 1B9.

Printed and bound in the United States of America

10 9 8 7 6 5 4 3 2 1

To Jane, remember there is no mountain too high for you to climb.

Acknowledgments

Although there is only one name on the cover of this book, and I take full responsibility for any errors, oversights, omissions or subjectivity, it would not have been possible to complete this project without the help of so many others. To those who shared thoughts, comments, observations and suggestions during endless long distance telephone calls, and to those who provided a place to sleep and a table to organize notes, I say thanks.

There are others who deserve more, but all that's within my power is to mention names. To Greg Weston in Whistler, who provided tireless research and words of encouragement when writer's block stilled my fingers on the keyboard, all while facing his own publishing deadline, I say lets go skiing pal. To John Colpitts and John Colebourn, whom I still owe much to from my previous life as editor of *Ski Canada* magazine, I say thanks for being there when it counted most. Bob Jamieson, the skiing cowboy who will always epitomize to me what this sport is all about; Paul Morrison, who not only provided the cover photograph, but friendship as well; Dave Steers, the soft-spoken technician who always made sure my equipment was better than I deserved; Alex Wilson, a friend, raconteur and the smoothest senior citizen on the slopes; Pat McGee and Diane Rhinehart, two former managing editors at *Ski Canada*, who always provided inspiration. And to that rarest of breeds, straight shooting marketing managers: Mike Duggan of Silver Star, Dave Gibson of Marmot Basin, Ken Fiske of Ski Norquay and Denis Boulanger of Mont Sutton.

And then too, there's Random House's Executive Editor, Doug Pepper, whom I thank for having faith; Sarah Davies, the editor who kept the wheels turning with patience and good humor; and Shaun Oakey, whose diligent copy editing brought it all together. Last, but by no means least, is Barbara, my wife and friend, who cracked the whip, patted my back and painstakingly checked every last detail. Without her, everything else would be for naught.

CONTENTS

All prices in this book are quoted in Canadian dollars.

THE FOLLOWING PRICE GUIDELINES HAVE BEEN USED:

All prices in this book are quoted in Canadian dollars.

"Where to Stay"
(based on one person per night without taxes)

Expensive	over $120
Moderate	$90 – $120
Inexpensive	under $90

Note: This guide applies unless the price is otherwise described (e.g., "per room" or "per person for 3 nights including meals").

"Where to Eat"
(based on a meal for two with one drink or glass of wine and without tip and taxes)

Expensive	over $80
Moderate	$50 – $80
Inexpensive	under $50

Every effort has been made to ensure the accuracy of information in this book, but changes do happen. If a hotel has upped its rates when you book your trip, or if last year's hottest disco has turned into a laundromat by the time you check it out, I apologize.

The following payment options are listed in the Where to Stay and Where to Eat sections:

Visa
MC (MasterCard)
Amex (American Express)
Diners (Diner's Club)
enRoute
CB (Carte Blanche)
Discover
JCB (Japan Credit Bureau)
CK (check)
T/CK (traveler's checks)

INTRODUCTION

There are more than 300 ski areas in Canada, and selecting the 20 that are detailed in this book was no easy process. It would have been simple to pick the 20 biggest, or to have picked 20 from mountainous British Columbia alone, but I wanted to provide a cross-section, a collection of resorts that support my contention that Canada's ski resorts are among the best in the world.

Of course such an abbreviated selection is bound to be subjective, and I make no apologies for that. What I have strived to present is a list of resorts I would be comfortable sending a skier like you to experience. There are as many reasons as there are resorts for picking a ski vacation destination, and only a few have anything to do with sliding down a slope. Cost, convenience, entertainment, ambience, access, weather and variety are all part of the equation. But what's perfect for me may not be best for you.

Skiers tend to be creatures of habit. A good experience at one resort brings us back for more. But in doing that, we often overlook other resorts that could give us a different but equally satisfying experience. Fortunately, Canada is blessed with an embarrassment of ski riches, and for every resort there's an overwhelming reason to sample its product. My selections will, I hope, widen your choice. Regardless of whether you are looking for the best ski instruction in the land, the longest runs, the deepest snow, the most torrid après-ski or the most romantic setting, there is something in this book to suit you.

HOW I PICKED THE RESORTS
The 20 resorts I chose are as varied as the Canadian character. They range from the very big (Whistler) to the very small (St-Sauveur); from the super-developed (Mont Ste-Anne) to the underdeveloped (Red Mountain). Some are so remote and isolated that nightlife is a black sky filled with dancing northern lights; others are as lively and as loaded with action as the most cosmopolitan urban center. They are expensive and ultra-cheap. They are owned and operated by international consortiums, small groups of businesspeople and families. Some are blessed with prodigious snowfalls, others rely almost entirely on the artificial variety. The weather conditions range from the ice-blue, sub-zero temperatures of Quebec to the shining skies of the Interior of B.C. and Alberta, to the temperate and capricious conditions of the west coast.

Despite all this diversity, however, they all have one common ingredient—a quality ski experience. Here's how that's measured.

I created 25 categories and nominated five top choices for each. A follow-up survey to the numerous people who helped with this book was factored in, and a 1–5 point system was applied to each resort, to provide the winner in each category. The categories were broad enough to give each resort a shot at scoring well, and the results (found on page xii–xiv) I believe endorse this system. In addition to the top 20, the last pages of this book contain a short list of 10 more resorts that are definitely worth a visit.

Here are the categories:
1. Top 5 for Vertical
2. Top 5 for Annual Snowfall
3. Top 5 for Snowmaking
4. Top 5 for Powder Skiing
5. Top 5 for Terrain Variety
6. Top 5 for Weather
7. Top 5 for Off-Piste
8. Top 5 for Glade Skiing
9. Top 5 for Giant Slalom Cruising
10. Top 5 for Skiing Days
11. Top 5 for Lack of Crowds
12. Top 5 for Alpine and Cross-Country Skiing
13. Top 5 for Scenery
14. Top 5 for Instruction
15. Top 5 for Lift Capacity
16. Top 5 for Ambience
17. Top 5 for Nightlife
18. Top 5 for Dining
19. Top 5 for Singles
20. Top 5 for Couples
21. Top 5 for Families
22. Top 5 for Luxury Accommodation
23. Top 5 for Small Inns
24. Top 5 for Urban Options
25. Top 5 for Ski to Your Door Convenience

SKI SURVEY RESULTS

TOP 5 FOR VERTICAL
1. Blackcomb
2. Whistler
3. Panorama
4. Skiing Louise
5. Red Mountain

TOP 5 FOR WEATHER
1. Silver Star
2. Big White
3. Red Mountain
4. Sunshine Village
5. Skiing Louise

TOP 5 FOR ANNUAL SNOWFALL
1. Red Mountain
2. Fernie Snow Valley
3. Sunshine Village
4. Blackcomb
5. Whistler

TOP 5 FOR OFF-PISTE
1. Skiing Louise
2. Whistler
3. Blackcomb
4. Red Mountain
5. Fernie Snow Valley

TOP 5 FOR SNOWMAKING
1. Nakiska
2. Mont Ste-Anne
3. Panorama
4. Gray Rocks
5. Stoneham

TOP 5 FOR GLADE SKIING
1. Mont Sutton
2. Marmot Basin
3. Red Mountain
4. Skiing Louise
5. Silver Star

TOP 5 FOR POWDER SKIING
1. Red Mountain
2. Fernie Snow Valley
3. Sunshine Village
4. Big White
5. Silver Star

TOP 5 FOR GIANT SLALOM CRUISING
1. Skiing Louise
2. Blackcomb
3. Whistler
4. Panorama
5. Kimberley Ski & Summer Resort

TOP 5 FOR TERRAIN VARIETY
1. Blackcomb
2. Skiing Louise
3. Red Mountain
4. Whistler
5. Marmot Basin

TOP 5 FOR SKIING DAYS
1. Mont Ste-Anne
2. Gray Rocks
3. Whistler
4. Blackcomb
5. Mont St-Sauveur

TOP 5 FOR LACK OF CROWDS
1. Red Mountain
2. Fernie Snow Valley
3. Kimberley Ski & Summer Resort
4. Panorama
5. Silver Star

TOP 5 FOR ALPINE AND CROSS-COUNTRY
1. Mont Ste-Anne
2. Silver Star
3. Mont St-Sauveur
4. Mont Tremblant
5. Mont Sutton

TOP 5 FOR SCENERY
1. Skiing Louise
2. Sunshine Village
3. Marmot Basin
4. Silver Star
5. Mont Tremblant

TOP 5 FOR INSTRUCTION
1. Gray Rocks
2. Mont St-Sauveur
3. Silver Star
4. Ski Norquay
5. Mont Sutton

TOP 5 FOR LIFT CAPACITY
1. Blackcomb
2. Whistler
3. Skiing Louise
4. Mont Ste-Anne
5. Sunshine Village

TOP 5 FOR AMBIENCE
1. Mont Tremblant
2. Silver Star
3. Stoneham
4. Skiing Louise
5. Mont Sutton

TOP 5 FOR NIGHTLIFE
1. Whistler
2. Blackcomb
3. Mont St-Sauveur
4. Ski Norquay
5. Mont Ste-Anne

TOP 5 FOR DINING
1. Mont Ste-Anne
2. Mont St-Sauveur
3. Stoneham
4. Mont Tremblant
5. Sunshine Village

TOP 5 FOR SINGLES
1. Whistler
2. Blackcomb
3. Ski Norquay
4. Mont Tremblant
5. Mont Ste-Anne

TOP 5 FOR COUPLES
1. Stoneham
2. Skiing Louise
3. Mont St-Sauveur
4. Mont Ste-Anne
5. Mont Sutton

TOP 5 FOR FAMILIES
1. Silver Star
2. Big White
3. Panorama
4. Mont Orford
5. Gray Rocks

TOP 5 FOR LUXURY ACCOMMODATION
1. Skiing Louise/ Château Lake Louise
2. Blackcomb/Château Whistler
3. Sunshine/Banff Springs
4. Nakiska/Lodge at Kananaskis
5. Stoneham/Hotel Stoneham

TOP 5 FOR SMALL INNS
1. Red Mountain/Ram's Head Inn
2. Skiing Louse/Skoki Lodge
3. Mont Ste-Anne/L'Aventure
4. Mont Tremblant/L'Escapade
5. Mont Sutton/La Capucine

TOP 5 FOR URBAN OPTIONS
1. Mont Ste-Anne
2. Stoneham
3. Mont Orford
4. Mont St-Sauveur
5. Whistler

TOP 5 FOR SKI TO YOUR DOOR CONVENIENCE
1. Silver Star
2. Big White
3. Sunshine Village
4. Whistler
5. Panorama

TOP 20 FINAL STANDINGS
1. Skiing Louise
2. Blackcomb
3. Whistler
4. Silver Star
5. Mont Ste-Anne
6. Red Mountain
7. Sunshine Village
8. Mont Tremblant
9. Big White
10. Marmot Basin
11. Fernie Snow Valley
12. Mont Sutton
13. Panorama
14. Stoneham
15. Mont Orford
16. Ski Norquay
17. Kimberley Ski & Summer Resort
18. Nakiska
19. Mont St-Sauveur
20. Gray Rocks

PLANNING YOUR SKI VACATION

Where to Go

This is your number-one consideration, but it's not a simple matter. What kind of skiing are you looking for? What kind of snow conditions? Are you comfortable skiing on loose, deep, powder snow, or do you prefer groomed runs? Is vertical or high-speed cruising your preference, or do you prefer shorter, punchier runs, or tree skiing? Are you traveling alone, as a couple, in a group or as a family? How much nightlife are you after?

You get the point. Pick your destination with the same care you would choose any other expensive purchase. Make a list of your priorities, decide on a budget, narrow your choice to the best three options, then shop around for the best deal.

When to Go

There are peak times at all major ski resorts: Christmas week, spring break and Easter week (if it's early in the year). Unless you have no choice, it's best to avoid these times. The resorts are always crowded, the prices always increase, and your choice of accommodation is often limited, especially if you don't book early enough. For many families, however, these are the only times when everyone can get away together, so try to make the best of it. Wherever you go will be busy, but you can avoid mega-crowds by choosing lesser-known destinations such as Red Mountain, Kimberley and Fernie. If you choose to go to one of the more popular areas, book early and be prepared to stand in line a lot.

Curiously, the least busy time at most areas is January. The post-Christmas bill-paying tends to slow things down, and often the best deals of the season are available at this time. Likewise, late in the season—early April—also is a good time to find reduced prices, smaller crowds and good weather.

Where to Stay

As a rule of thumb, the closer your accommodation is to the slopes, the more expensive it will be. You can usually save a bundle by walking five minutes to the slopes each morning.

The choice between hotels or condos is primarily a matter of whether you enjoy being catered to or don't mind making meals at home. A condo can be more comfortable and spacious; families and large groups find condo living easier. And watch the figures—condo units may appear to be more expensive on a per-night basis, but divided by the number of occupants, they often work out cheaper than a hotel room.

Here are some useful questions to help you decide where to stay

• Location. Will you be renting a car? If you have transportation, then you can pick accommodation farther afield. If you don't want either the hassle or cost of a car, stick to accommodation within walking distance of the lifts.

• Size. How much time do you plan to spend in your accommodation? If it is only to sleep, why pay for a party palace? How many bathrooms do you need? Six people lining up for one bathroom can turn avid skiers ugly.

Ever noticed that everything with a bed, toilet and a window in ski country is advertised as "bright, spacious and the ultimate in luxury"? Be warned: ski country developers have added new meaning to the concept of compact living space. Before you book, ask for the square footage of the hotel room, suite or condo.

• Amenities. Do they have hot tubs, saunas, spas, exercise rooms? If you don't want them, why pay for them? Do they have family games rooms and other amusements for the kids? (Also an important warning signal for those who want to keep away from kids.)

• Lift tickets. Are they included? If not, insist on it. Usually hotels and lodges will get a better deal than you will on lift tickets because they make a bulk purchase. Savings are usually passed on to guests.

• Packages. Do they have multi-night rates? Usually a three-to-five-day package is cheaper than the single-night rate, yet few places will point this out. Do they have special deals with airlines, car rental companies, etc.?

• Taxes. Are they included? Remember that various taxes can add up to 25 percent to your bill.

• Ground transportation. Do they provide shuttle service from the airport (a lot do, but few mention it) or from the airport bus drop-off point? After a long flight, the last thing you want is to haul a lot of luggage more than 10 feet.

- Parking. Do they have it? Does it cost extra?

- Toys. What extras are you looking for? If they say they have a pool, is it indoors? Do they have a dining room, coffee shop or convenience store? Laundry facilities?

How to Go

For those who don't believe getting there is half the fun, a package tour is attractive, and not just because of the convenience. There are considerable savings to be had from all-inclusive package deals, which combine airfare, hotel, lift tickets and meals in one neat and tidy package.

Today's packages allow you to pick your departure day, select your preferred accommodation and enjoy your own company if you wish. You can also modify many of the standard packages. For instance, you can sometimes upgrade your accommodation, arrange for a rental car or secure a meal plan. Generally speaking, the more all-inclusive a package is, the more money you will save.

Regardless of whether you make your own custom arrangements or go the package route, get answers to these questions before confirming the trip.

- Flight times. What times does your flight depart and return? That ultra-cheap red-eye special may mean you lose a day of skiing at one end of your week, or maybe even both. Likewise, an early-morning departure on your last day could eat into your skiing time.

- Shuttles and transfers. Are they included in your package deal? If making your own arrangements, check with either your hotel or the airline to find out frequency, time and cost. There's nothing worse than hanging around a hotel for several hours waiting for a bus.

- Car rentals. Once you've decided if you need one, shop for the best deal. Always arrange for an airport pick-up and return, and if you plan to drop the car off at your destination, find out about drop-off charges—they can be $100 or more in some cases. Rent from a city or airport outlet—car rentals at ski areas tend to be limited and more expensive. Reserve ahead if you can, and make sure you ask for a winterized car with a ski rack.

• Occupancy. When getting price quotes, make sure you understand clearly the number of guests in each room. Often the lowest price quoted means four to a room—and sometimes you can end up sharing with strangers. If privacy, not price, is your priority, make that clear when booking.

POINTERS ON PACKING FOR YOUR TRIP

What to Take

• Ski pants and jacket. Take two if your wardrobe permits, and remember that a one-piece suit, while the ultimate in comfort, is generally inflexible when the temperature bounces up and down like your knees on a mogul run. Two-piece suits—or suit systems as they are more commonly called—are better, but you can add versatility to your ensemble by packing a shell or wind jacket, wind pants, vest or stretch ski pants.

• Sweaters. Wool is preferable. Remember they can do double duty with your off-slope wear, so color-coordinate if possible.

• Turtlenecks. One a day is a luxury, one for every other day is refreshing, one for every four or five days will offend your companions.

• Socks. A pair for every two days is the minimum unless you're going to wash them out every night. But please, no sweatsocks, work socks or dress socks—at least not for skiing—as these types of socks can bunch up inside your ski boots and cause discomfort. Include a pair of silk sock liners for cold feet.

• Sweatsuit. Useful for lounging, dashing to the outdoor sauna, sleeping in or doubling as extra-long-underwear on extra-cold days.

• Gloves, goggles, tuques, neck warmers, head bands. Two of each, if for no other reason than it will make you a popular person when a less-organized companion comes looking for a spare.

- Footwear. Dress shoes do not cut it at most ski resorts. Instead take sneakers, deck shoes, lightweight hiking boots or something that doubles as a casual dress shoe.

- Casual clothing. Your choice entirely, but remember that ski resorts are casual places and a Burberry trenchcoat or designer evening wear will likely go unused. Conversely, if the height of your sartorial elegance is a "sleep is for wimps" sweatshirt, you might feel a touch out of place in a swanky restaurant. Also remember that you'll spend two-thirds of your waking hours in ski clothing.

- Bathing suit. My unofficial survey suggests this is the most frequently overlooked item, and rental suits are just a tad tacky. Even if your hotel doesn't have a pool, it may have a sauna or jacuzzi.

And if Room Permits

- Portable sound. A Walkman is a nice personal addition, but it's also anti-social, so consider a small portable tape player.

- Repair items. A Swiss army knife is the most indispensable, but also consider a small multi-headed screwdriver, vise grips, bastard file, duct tape and elastic shock straps. These items may seem a bit survivalist in nature, but the tape can repair ripped ski clothes or luggage, the shock cords can secure a wonky ski rack, and the Swiss army knife can do almost anything, including open a bottle of wine.

- Games and other diversions. Boardgames, cards and reading material all help pass the time for those not of the party-till-you-pass-out persuasion. And don't forget a camera, film and spare batteries.

- Sundry items. Along with your basic toiletries, it's useful to include: aspirins, antihistamines, band-aids, a tensor bandage and ice pack. Don't forget sunglasses, sun block and an alarm clock.

What to Take It In

Soft luggage is a must. Forget hard-sided suitcases. These are all you will need to tote to the slopes:

- Duffle or equipment bag. Your largest piece of luggage, and in most cases bigger is better. A sturdy waterproof model will cost you between $80 and $120, but it will outlast most of your ski equipment. Look for quality nylon or vulcanized canvas. Pay attention to seams, stitching and welding. And make sure it has strong carrying handles that go all the way around the back of the bag and are not just stitched to the top. A sturdy shoulder strap is also essential. A full-length, two-way, heavy-duty zipper is a must, and a small inside pocket is a bonus. Several models come with large pockets at either end designed to hold ski boots, but use them for other items or your bag will weigh too much.

- Boot bag. I'm always amused, when watching luggage clattering around the airport luggage carousel, at the number of unprotected pairs of boots that come tumbling down. Not only is there potential for damage to the boots but the owners are missing out on some great extra luggage space. Invest in a good boot bag and you'll never have to agonize over which of your five pairs of goggles to pack. When buying a boot bag, think big, and definitely avoid those nifty-looking ones in the shape of a boot; they may be stylish, but there's not much room inside. Avoid boot bags with small openings, and make sure there's a strong shoulder strap. Once your boots are stowed you can cram the rest of the space with everything from tool kits to footwear.

- Ski bag. Like unprotected boots, unprotected skis are a no-no. Make sure the bag is sturdy, with a full-length zipper and a shoulder strap. It should be large enough to take skis *and* poles, and the secret here is to use all the extra space to pack clothing. Sweaters, pants, jackets and almost anything else can be wrapped around the skis. Not only does this afford extra protection but it makes use of an incredible amount of extra storage space.

- Day pack. This is your most important piece of luggage, and serves double duty. It doesn't need to be too large, but it should have multiple outside pockets. Use it to pack all your personal items—tickets, passport, valuables, medications, sunglasses, etc.—for traveling, and at the resort it's essential for carrying your lunch, refreshments and things like sunscreen, camera and goggles.

And How to Take It

• Don't waste space inside your boots or other footwear. Stuff them with breakable items—shampoo, cassette tapes, etc.—and top off with socks.

• Roll, don't fold, bulky items such as jackets and sweaters as tightly as you would a sleeping bag, then hold them together with small straps.

• Use bags inside bags. Small nylon accessory bags are good for keeping items separate and easy to find.

• Wear, don't pack, your bulkiest items.

• Keep all hard or breakable items in the center of your biggest bag to afford extra protection.

• Wrap your skis and poles with ski pants, turtlenecks, long underwear. Don't overlook the cavity around the ski tips; there's always room for footwear or gloves.

• Load all your miscellaneous footwear in your boot bag. And wrap each pair in a plastic bag. This helps keep them organized, and is useful on the return journey when some may be wet or caked in dirt.

• When you're all packed, tape over the ends of the zippers with duct tape to prevent pilfering or accidental opening. A small lock does the same job.

• Finally, make sure you are able to carry everything at once—if only for a short distance.

OTHER TIPS FOR TRAVELING SKIERS

By Air

Most airlines accept skis as part of your regular luggage, but at many airports they have to be checked in at the special services desk and retrieved at your destination in an area separate from the main luggage carousel, so allow a little extra time at both ends of your trip. Make sure you have an identification tag on your ski bag. Carry your boots on the plane as hand luggage rather than checking them through. Lost or delayed skis are easy to replace with a rental pair, but lost boots are a bigger problem. Even if you can rent a pair, they are not likely to fit as well as your own.

By Train

Shipping skis by train can be a hassle. Via Rail requires that skis be checked in at the station 24 hours before departure. Some trains do not have baggage cars, and often your skis will end up traveling on a separate train. If you don't give Via or Amtrak enough time to properly handle your skis, they might arrive later than you do. Check with Via Rail or Amtrak for instructions.

Rental Cars

Ski luggage takes up a lot of room, so if more than two persons are traveling together you may find that a sub-compact or a compact car doesn't have enough room for all your gear. When booking a rental car, ask for a model with a large trunk area. Also request a vehicle equipped with either snow tires or all-weather radials, and if you are traveling into isolated mountain regions, ask about the availability of tire chains. Make sure you request a ski rack— don't wait until you get to your pick-up point, or you may discover that there are no racks in stock—and keep in mind that most racks on rental cars are flimsy contraptions that won't handle your overstuffed ski bags very easily. Take along two or three elastic shock cords to help secure ski bags to the rack.

TIPS FOR VISITORS ENTERING CANADA

Travel between the United States and Canada is easy. You will have to clear customs, but usually all that entails is showing some valid identification and answering a few basic questions about your citizenship, destination and length of stay in Canada.

For visitors from elsewhere, a passport is necessary. If you are arriving in a rental car via the United States, make sure you have the proper rental documents and any additional insurance required by the rental company. Canadians cannot rent a car in the United States and cross into Canada with the vehicle. Americans driving into Canada in their own car should carry a valid licence, insurance and ownership papers.

All speed limits in Canada are posted in metric; 100 km/h is equal to 60 mph.

MONEY

All prices in this book are quoted in Canadian dollars.
Most businesses will accept U.S. dollars, but their exchange rate may not be as good as you will find at Canadian banks and trust companies. If you arrive with other currency, exchange it into Canadian dollars at the airport or at a bank in a major center; be aware that some small town branches of major chartered banks will not exchange foreign currency. Most establishments will take traveler's checks that are in U.S. or Canadian dollars.

FURTHER INFORMATION
The following provincial tourism offices can provide further information about the regions or destinations in this book.

Tourism Alberta
4th Floor
10155 – 102 St
Edmonton, Alberta
T5J 4L6
Tel toll-free (U.S. & Canada) 1-800-661-8888

British Columbia Ministry of Tourism
802 – 865 Hornby St
Vancouver, B.C.
V6Z 2G3
Tel toll-free (U.S. & Canada) 1-800-663-6000

Tourism Québec   or   Tourism Québec
20 Queen St West   2 Place Québec
Suite 1504   Bureau 336
Box 13   Québec City, Quebec
Toronto, Ontario   G1R 2B5
M5H 3S3   Tel (418) 643-8499
Tel (416) 977-6060   Toll-free (U.S. & Canada) 1-800-363-7777

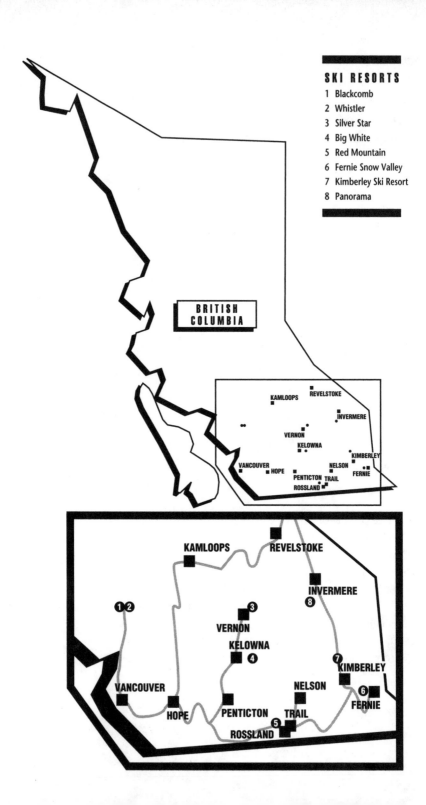

SKI RESORTS

1 Blackcomb
2 Whistler
3 Silver Star
4 Big White
5 Red Mountain
6 Fernie Snow Valley
7 Kimberley Ski Resort
8 Panorama

BRITISH COLUMBIA

KAMLOOPS REVELSTOKE
INVERMERE
VERNON
KELOWNA
KIMBERLEY
NELSON
VANCOUVER HOPE
PENTICTON TRAIL FERNIE
ROSSLAND

KAMLOOPS REVELSTOKE
INVERMERE
VERNON
KELOWNA
KIMBERLEY
NELSON
VANCOUVER
HOPE PENTICTON TRAIL FERNIE
ROSSLAND

BRITISH COLUMBIA

BRITISH COLUMBIA

Of all the myths common to a land as vast as Canada, perhaps few are more persistent than the belief that western skiing is confined to the Rocky Mountains. To be sure, the Rockies are an impressive chunk of terrain, stretching 215 mi (345 km) along the border of Alberta and B.C. But to the west are range upon range of craggy snow-covered peaks that pierce the western sky in the same dramatic fashion as their better-known Rocky Mountain cousins.

Their names echo a pioneer past, but their geological ancestry goes back many millennia, when massive volcanic movement shaped the rugged Cordillera that forms the twisted backbone of the North American continent from Panama to the Bering Strait. The Monashees, Purcells, Selkirks, Kootenays and the Coast Mountains today provide an abundance of some of the best—and least-known—ski resorts in North America.

It was only a little more than a century ago that the first explorers punched their way through the narrow passes that allowed access to the vast tracts of wilderness that roll west to the Pacific Ocean and north to the Arctic Circle. And it's only in the past 20 years that explorers in Gore-Tex, not buckskin, toting skis, not muskets, have discovered the white bounty that these mountains hold.

With its land mass of 366,000 sq mi (948 000 km²), this western-most province is large enough to contain the traditional alpine nations of Switzerland, France, Italy and Austria. It also yields more alpine peaks over 9,000 ft (2750 m) than anywhere outside the Himalayas. What characterizes British Columbia is its diversity of regions distinctive in their climate, geography and vegetation. This province offers coastal archipelagoes, dense coniferous and boreal forests, extensive lake and river systems, mountains and glaciers and the semi-arid conditions of the southern Interior. With 16,750 mi (27 000 km) of coastline and more than a thousand coastal islands, B.C. presents an astonishing natural smorgasbord that features fiords and hot springs, waterfalls and deserts, glaciers and rain forest, grizzly bears and eagles—and range upon range of mountains fit to be skied.

The skiing in B.C. mirrors this tantalizing topography and weather with a mix that ranges from the heavy wet snow of the coast to the light dry powder of the Interior. When the moist Pacific air clashes with the outer Coast Mountains, the ensuing precipitation not only helps nourish the largest trees on earth but also provides coastal mountain ski resorts such as Whistler with some of the most prodigious snowfalls on the continent—sometimes topping 400 in (1000 cm). As this air moves east across the fertile lowland valleys and then rises to the summit of the craggy ranges that block the way to the open prairies, it converts the moisture it carries into the lighter, drier snow of the Interior region. And it's there that you find the snow-kissed resorts of the Okanagan, the Kootenays and yes, at last, the Rockies.

Just as the resorts are shaped by their geographic components, so too are the cities and towns of the valleys. Insulated by geography and born of circumstances, their mining, logging and other natural-resource heritage is being supplanted by a modern-day resource—tourism. Kelowna, midway up the Okanagan Valley, is one of Canada's fastest-growing "alternative lifestyle" cities. Kimberley, its mines slowly falling silent, has learned quickly that steep mountains and deep snow can be mined in a different way.

You can't call them ski towns, exactly, at least not in the European sense, but whether it be Rossland and Red Mountain, Vernon and Silver Star, or Kelowna and Big White, the link between resort and community is like that of the valleys to the peaks. The creature comforts of the ski resorts notwithstanding, it behooves you to explore the nearby towns and cities.

This is best done by car, unless you can charter a chopper for a week. And as you'll discover in the following pages many of these areas are within a scenic one- to two-hour drive of each other, making it possible over the course of a week's ski vacation to sample as many as four ski areas.

After a look at the network of highways that snake their way across a map of B.C., the task of getting from point A to B may seem daunting, and indeed the mountain barriers that are nirvana to skiers force creative use of switchbacks and narrow climbing passes. But despite the natural hazards of rock falls, landslides, washouts and reduced visibility, B.C.'s major highways are remarkably trouble-free—a testament to the largest fleet of highway maintenance vehicles of any jurisdiction on the continent.

And things have been made easier with some recent improvements. The newly built toll-road, the Coquihalla Highway, cuts in half the driving time between Vancouver and the Okanagan Valley. And while the Sea-to-Sky highway up to Whistler is terminally under repair, the delays are shorter and the slides less frequent.

Any journey into the regions discussed in the following pages should be tackled only with careful planning and steady driving. It's easy to be lulled by the bucolic, snow-free lowlands, but as the whine of the engine signals a long, slow climb through yet another alpine pass, a blizzard can materialize around the next blind corner, and the road become as slick as a sheet of ice. But don't let this put you off. Explore you must if you are ever to know the full measure of B.C.'s skiing wonders, and it's easy to carve out slices of this wilderness pie starting with the resorts of the Coast Mountains, then moving east to the Okanagan Valley, the Kootenays and finally the B.C. Rockies.

THE COAST MOUNTAINS

WHISTLER
Box 67
Whistler, B.C.
V0N 1B0
Tel (604) 932-3434; from
Vancouver 685-1007

HOW TO GET THERE
By Plane: Whistler is 75 mi
(120 km) northeast of
Vancouver. Vancouver
International Airport is
served by major airlines, with
connections from major
centers.

By Car: Car rentals are
available at Vancouver
Airport and in downtown
Vancouver. The drive to
Whistler is approximately
2 ½ hours. From downtown
Vancouver, take the Lions
Gate Bridge into North
Vancouver, then follow signs
for Hwy 99, also known as
the Sea-to-Sky Highway.
(Chains are sometimes
mandatory.)

By Bus: Perimeter
Transportation runs three
trips daily Mon to Thurs and
four trips daily Fri to Sun
from Vancouver Airport to
Whistler; for reservations call
(604) 266-5386. From the
main bus terminal downtown
(at Dunsmuir and Beatty),
Maverick Coach Lines (604-
662-8051) runs three daily
shuttles to Whistler.

By Train: B.C. Rail (604-984-
5246) runs a daily service
from North Vancouver to
Whistler. A shuttle bus runs
from the Vancouver bus

It's not easy to sidestep the superlatives when speaking of Whistler. The best. The biggest. The steepest. The highest. The most expensive. The name Whistler encompasses the village, the resort municipality, two mighty mountains, three glaciers, five alpine bowls and myriad other elements that combine to make this the best-known resort in North America.

Even regular visitors to this alpine playground are hard-pressed to keep apace of the dizzying development as, in 25 short years, some $600 million has been spent at Whistler and nearby Blackcomb to create some 200 trails and runs in a peerless pairing of the two highest lift-serviced verticals on the continent. Augmented by one of the largest high-speed lift systems money can buy, this fleet of quad chairs and a 10-passenger gondola can transport 40,000 skiers an hour to the twin summits that rise shoulder-to-shoulder on either side of the Fitzsimmons valley and offer an unsurpassed 3,657 acres (1462 ha) of skiable terrain. And that is just the tip of the mountain, for beyond that lie the back bowls and the glaciers that give Whistler and Blackcomb the only genuine year-round skiing in Canada.

The sheer scope of all this skiing is apt to leave the expert breathless, the first-time visitor overwhelmed and the long-time local still discovering new terrain. It's a true measure of these mega-resorts that discovery lies around every corner, and a trail map is as indispensable as your skis.

All this is quite recent. It was only in 1965, when a group of local businessmen formed Garibaldi Lifts and opened the original gondola, that thoughts of a complementary base village surfaced. Today, the village of Whistler is a bustling community of some 6,000 residents with its own fire department, police terminal to the train station. The Whistler train station is serviced by both bus and taxi.

By Helicopter: Air service to Whistler from Vancouver Airport or downtown Vancouver is available on Canadian Helicopters. Call (604) 276-7670.

WHISTLER— STATISTICALLY SPEAKING

Base Elevation:
2,140 ft (652 m)

Summit Elevation:
7,160 ft (2182 m)

Vertical Drop:
5,020 ft (1530 m)

Skiable Terrain:
3,657 acres (1462 ha)

Number of Trails: 100+

Longest Run: 6.8 mi (11 km)

Lifts & Capacity: 1 gondola, 3 quads, 3 triples, 2 doubles, 2 T-bars, 1 platter; 22,295 skiers per hour

Daily Lift Ticket:
Adult $40
Weekly: Adult $195
(dual-mountain, 5 days)

Annual Snowfall:
345 in (860 cm)

No. Days Skiing 91–92: 150

Snowmaking: 1%

Terrain Mix:
N 25%, I 55%, E 20%

Snow Phone: 932-4191

force, banks, doctors, school, freight depot, chapel, underground parking, dog catcher and yes, sad to say, even its own parking enforcement officers.

For visitors, there are more than 10,000 beds, ranging from the ritzy new Château Whistler to more humble pension or B&B shelters. Condos and cabins crowd both sides of the highway, and helicopters prowl the sky bringing the well-heeled from Vancouver. Restaurants, bars, bistros, discos and other eating and drinking emporiums are prolific enough to warrant their own Yellow Pages, and the choice runs the gamut from sushi to sandwiches, pasta to pizza, Mediterranean to California chic. If you have a taste for something, chances are you'll find it in Whistler. And it doesn't stop there. The buy-till-you-overdraft crowd can browse boutiques searching for that ever so darling something ranging from mink-lined after-ski duds to souvenirs for every taste.

Of course, all this lavish development does come at a price. Whistler is rapidly becoming known as the most expensive ski resort in the country. If the spirit is willing and the bank balance buoyant, you can sleep away the night in four-star splendor for $500, dally over dinner for $100 or more, or pay full retail mark-up on everything from skis to designer clothing.

Fortunately, the wealthy are not the only visitors welcome at Whistler. Regular folk still make the scene, and bargains can be found. But remember, the best does have its price.

THE SKIING

As with many things as Whistler, deciding where to start skiing depends entirely on what the Coast Mountains serve up in the way of weather. With the series of micro-climates that layer themselves from the valley to the summit, whither-the-weather, so goes your level of skiing enjoyment. The first commandment of those in the know is not to be intimidated by what you see outside your window first thing in the a.m. What you see is not always what you get.

In fact, don't let anything about the weather put you off. I spent a total of 17 days in three separate visits before seeing the peak from the valley, but once our group broke free of the damp, clammy confines of the Fitzsimmons valley, the skiing was, almost without fail, exceptional. It's those micro-climates, which dry the moisture as you rise up to Whistler's summit. Until Gore-Tex, Entrant and other breathable waterproof fabrics made the scene, it was de rigueur to wrap a plastic garbage bag around your body for the initial 2,000-foot (600-m) ride up. The moisture of the valley undergoes a miraculous transformation as it rises, and rain in the village can translate into wet snow by mid-station, heavier snow as you approach the summit, then finally the lighter snow of the upper elevations.

So if you wake up to the sound of rain, remember that up above it all is snow, precisely what you've come for, and it falls in abundance on Whistler Mountain, some 350 in (860 cm) annually, and it gives Whistler a six-month-long ski season (excluding the summertime option of skiing the high glaciers). Remember, too, that the damp air is warm off the Pacific Ocean. You will not encounter the biting cold of the more easterly Rockies or the sub-zero temperatures of, say, Quebec. Even in the high alpine regions in the coldest part of the winter, the temperature seldom dips below 5° F (–15° C), while in the sheltered lower part of the mountain the winter average is around 23° F (–5° C). Leave your down duds, your face masks and your boot heaters at home. At Whistler, you just won't need them.

HOW TO SKI WHISTLER

To reach the summit, take one of the two high-speed quads from the south village up to the Roundhouse, or grab the 10-passenger gondola from the main village. Both rides allow the shaky to get off at approximately mid-mountain, and likewise skiing down from the Roundhouse doesn't mean you have to exit back down at base, because you can load up again at the mid-station mark of the quad chairs, or the Olympic station on the gondola. The wisdom of this is readily apparent if the snow on the lower half of the mountain is the heavy west coast muck that grabs at your skis like a dog to a bone.

The bowls will beckon from the Roundhouse via either the Peak Chair or the two high-alpine T-bars, and although the locals with the case-hardened thighs will often search out the untracked snow early in the day, visitors are advised to stretch the kinks out of their lower extremities by taking one of the high-speed cruising runs. Upper Franz's Run starts about 220 yd (200 m) below the Roundhouse, and while it's tagged only as a "more difficult" blue run, its natural steepness will accelerate you to warp speed that will force you to keep your head up, and your edges set, especially as you hit the rolls and dips that this natural fall-line run features. If you catch the rhythm and you feel you can go on forever, connect to Lower Franz's just below mid-station, and ride the wave all the way to the Whistler Creek base.

You can also reach the upper part of Upper Franz's by riding the Peak Chair to Whistler's true summit, then either take the black diamond chutes of the Whistler bowl, or take a straight shot down the less difficult Highway 86, which parallels the mountain's south boundary line. If you choose the Highway route, keep a sharp eye for the extreme right turn at the edge of the western boundary.

If you're feeling particularly frisky, drop down the Bagel Bowl, just shy of that point, then reconnect with Highway 86 just a few hundred yards before picking up Franz's again.

You can coast on down to the base, or make a cut to the right and pick up the Redline Quad for a ride back to the Roundhouse.

If at that point you feel inclined to move your internal speedometer up a notch or two, consider the Upper Downhill, a world-class World Cup run that implores you to carry as much speed as you dare. It too will deposit you at the Whistler Creek base area if you connect from the Upper Downhill to the Lower Downhill.

Whistler is a mountain with enough advanced skiing for even the most demonic denizens of the steep, yet there is terrain aplenty for the novice. More than one beginner has taken those first tentative turns on the gently sloping green runs that skirt the steep pitches and carry the novice safely to the bottom of the mountain. If that's your category, don't shy away from the scenic ride to the Roundhouse; just watch the signs and follow such gentle runs as Papoose, Sidewinder, Foxy Hollow, Mom's Run and Pony Trail.

And remember, it's impossible to groom the entire mountain, so check the daily grooming reports, which are posted at hotels, ski shops and ticket wickets.

Novices/Low Intermediates

Take the gondola to Olympic mid-station (first semi-stop on the way up), then traverse over to Olympic Chair. From there pick up either Upper Fantastic or Foxy Hollow; both are wide and flat and return to the Olympic Chair. (Don't bother fighting the gondola lines after each run.) You can also take the gondola to the Roundhouse station. From there go left to Ego Bowl and Green Acres to the Green Chair. These wide, gentle and well-groomed runs are listed as intermediate but are quite easy.

A note: For the novice, the timid or the less aggressive significant other, it's not necessary to ski in slow-motion isolation. If you pick the right green runs you can move at your own pace yet still rendezvous with the gang for the ride back up, or join them for a break at the Roundhouse. You might only connect every second run or so, but that's better than waving goodbye after breakfast and not meeting up again until the end of the day.

Intermediates

Take the gondola to the Roundhouse station, go left from there and pick up Ego Bowl, Jolly Green Giant or Green Acres (all return to the Green Chair). Or head right from the Roundhouse to Little Red Run, Fisheye, Upper Franz's and back down to the Redline Quad. These are great cruising runs usually with light powder.

Experts

Take the gondola to the Roundhouse, then the Peak Chair to the summit where almost anything is steep and bumpy. Try the Whistler Bowl for true vertical. If the weather's bad and the Peak Chair isn't operating, from the Roundhouse pick up the Ridge Run or Chunky's. From the Black Chair, try Seppo's.

Powder Pursuit

Finding the best powder runs on Whistler depends almost entirely on the wind. If a certain chute happens to be out of the wind on a given day, the powder will be deep and light. If it's in the wind, it can be like turning in cement and impossible to ski on anything other than steep pitches.

In general, if the peak is open after a fresh snowfall, go there. Stop at the patrollers shack at the unload area and ask for directions to the best safe powder. Remember: this is a heavy avalanche area. If the Peak Chair is not open because of wind or poor visibility, take the T-bars. Some of the best powder skiing on the mountain is on the runs right beside them.

BEST TOP TO BOTTOM

There's no point in having a mile of vertical and only skiing a thousand feet of it. Take a deep breath and go for the full shot. Even intermediates not wanting to tempt fate on the Peak Chair can ski well over 6 mi (10 km) from the Roundhouse to the base on either side of the mountain.

For Intermediates

1. Gondola to Peak Chair. Highway 86 to Upper Franz's to Lower Franz's all the way to Whistler Creek.
2. Gondola to Roundhouse. Ridge Run to Green Acres to Olympic all the way to the village.

For Experts

1. Gondola to Peak Chair. Turn left off the Peak Chair, drop over the lip at the Saddle into Whistler Glacier, pass the base of the Peak Chair and go on to Franz's Meadows to Upper and Lower Franz's all the way down to Whistler Creek.
2. Gondola to Peak Chair. Take Highway 88 to West Bowl, back to Highway 88 to Upper Franz's to Dave Murray Downhill to Whistler Creek. Plan on it taking the better part of an hour, not including a well-deserved beer break at Dusty's.

BLACKCOMB MOUNTAIN

4545 Blackcomb Way
Box 98
Whistler, B.C.
V0N 1B0
Tel (604) 932-3141

BLACKCOMB— STATISTICALLY SPEAKING

Base Elevation:
2,214 ft (675 m)

Summit Elevation:
7,494 (2284 m)

Vertical Drop:
5,280 ft (1610 m)

Skiable Terrain:
3,340 acres (1336 ha)

Number of Trails: 91

Longest Run: 7 mi (11.2 km)

Lifts & Capacity: 4 quads,
5 tri-chairs, 1 double,
2 T-bars;
23,850 skiers per hour

Daily Lift Ticket: $42

Weekly: $180 (5 days); dual-mountain $195

Annual Snowfall:
334 in (835 cm)

No. Days Skiing 91–92: 150

Snowmaking: 1%

Terrain Mix:
N 20%, I 55%, E 25%

Snow Phone: 932-4211

THE SKIING

Many people observe that Whistler—the ski area and the village—would not be what it is today were it not for the emergence of Blackcomb, the mountain that rises 7,494 ft (2284 m) above the Fitzsimmons valley and claims the highest lift-serviced vertical in North America. Undeniably, the head-to-head competition that these two resorts embarked on in the early 1980s produced the most dynamic development race since the days of bear trap bindings, and the beneficiaries of all this mega-buck spending are the skiers. Keep in mind, though, that if Blackcomb stood alone it would still offer more skiing than virtually any other resort in the country.

Fully half of Whistler's 6,997 acres (2800 ha) of lift-serviced terrain is on Blackcomb, and if you do manage to try each of the 91 marked trails, the skiing on the Horstman and Blackcomb glaciers offers yet another dimension.

The cut and marked runs that cover Blackcomb are generally fall-line runs. That is, they follow the natural path that the vertical pitch provides, but they are also wide, sweeping boulevards of meticulously groomed snow. The width and the grooming are generally a concession to the 1980s skier, a pampered creature who wants maximum mileage for the effort. As a result many skiers tend to carry a tad too much speed for their ability, and series of curves, drops, rolls and pitches have been created to temper this inclination.

Fact is, you could ski Blackcomb for an entire ski season and still find new and interesting ways down the mountain. And like Whistler, the way you ski it is to a large degree dependent on the weather.

HOW TO SKI BLACKCOMB

A hint: On weekends, get to Seventh Heaven before 9 a.m. or wait until after 11 a.m. unless you like lift lines. The exception is on powder days—it will always open later than the lower mountain because of avalanche control. On windy or low-visibility days, avoid the Seventh Heaven area altogether, even if it is open.

Novices

Take the Wizard to Solar Coaster and pick up Easy Out (stay to the right) to Lower Catskinner to Catskinner Chair. (Note: The Catskinner Chair is one of the least traveled on the mountain, with some excellent runs for all levels from beginner to cruisers to diamond bumps. It's a good area for groups of varying abilities. You can meet back at the chair after each run.)

Take the Wizard to Solar Coaster. Pick up Cruiser to Wishbone to Jersey Cream Chair if you're a modest intermediate. Better skiers in the group can head for Walrus Knob to Blowdown and meet back at the Jersey Cream Chair.

Intermediates

Take Solar Coaster up, then head for Cruiser right off the back of the Rendezvous Lodge. This run is exactly what its name implies—4,100 vertical ft (1250 m) of groomed cruising with no flats.

Head up to Seventh Heaven and try Southern Comfort.

Take the Jersey Cream Chair and follow Jersey Cream Bowl to Cougar Milk.

From Seventh Heaven take the Glacier T-bar, then a short climb to the Blackcomb Glacier. One of the largest bowls in North America, this is for fair-weather days and advanced intermediates only, but it's a must-ski run for anyone who can handle the terrain. Remember, if you get into trouble, traverse—and watch out for icy conditions at the ski-out at the bottom.

Experts

On a Powder Day

Ride the Solar Coaster, then head for Choker, Cruiser or Jersey Cream. These are smooth runs but with enough vertical for powder.

Take Crystal Ridge Lift to Straight Shot, White Light or Trapline. All are steep, with rolling bumps and generally good powder.

From Seventh Heaven take the Showcase T-bar and then head for the

Blackcomb Glacier—only on fair-weather days. But pray you get an opportunity to ski this if only to experience the vistas and the sheer size of it all.

For Bumps
Take Jersey Cream Chair, then pick Blowdown, Overbite or Staircase. Kiss your knees goodbye—more than 2,000 vertical ft (610 m) of bumps on any of them.

Take Solar Coaster to Catskinner to Gearjammer. Steep bumps; avoid them on icy days.

Double Diamonds
Seventh Heaven lift to Saudan Couloir. This is the braggart's paradise of Blackcomb. Mandatory for anyone who can ski it. While you catch your breath at the bottom, look back up and try to imagine the 300 crazies who ski it every spring as a downhill course. The daring can also try Pakalolo and Sylvain. Both are steeper than Saudan.

BEST TOP TO BOTTOM
The highest vertical in North America demands everyone ski it all at least once—if only to brag about it. There are two good ways down.

Take Wizard to Solar Coaster to Seventh Heaven. Take Horstman Glacier to Hot Rocks Traverse (keep right at bottom of Glacier T-bar) and go hard right at the Crystal Hut to Ridge Runner connecting to Rock and Roll, Short Horn, Cruiser and finally Merlin to the bottom of Wizard Express.

Or, from Seventh Heaven Lift take Horstman, then cut across under the Jersey Cream Chair to Jersey Cream to Zig-Zag to Cruiser.

WHISTLER OR BLACKCOMB: WHICH IS THE BEST TO SKI?
Don't even bother to ask the locals—you'll get as many different answers with as many different reasons from as many different people as you ask. Ski both and decide for yourself. Unless you are absolutely wedded to one mountain or another, your best bet is a one- or five-day dual mountain pass, good on either mountain on any day. The cost is only about 5 percent more than a regular pass for one mountain. And it never fails: buy a pass for one mountain and all the sunshine (and the friends you met the night before) will be on the other mountain.

A WORD OF CAUTION

Whistler and Blackcomb offer some of the best and safest skiing anywhere in the world. But remember they are mountains—not hills! And they come with all the perils that rugged, high-altitude terrain can feature. Use a little caution and common sense and keep the following in mind.

- Boundary Lines. Don't even think about crossing them. The first few hundred yards beyond the boundaries may look like the best snow in the world, but the hidden sheer cliffs below them are fatal. These areas are not patrolled, and anyone skiing them is (a) stupid; (b) will be barred from the mountain; (c) probably won't be found if lost or injured; (d) will be charged the full fare—we're talking thousands of dollars—for rescue, if there's anything left of you worth saving.

- Two signs to pay strict attention to:
  - "Closed—Avalanche Danger!" Keep out, blasting may be in progress.
  - "Avalanche Prone Area." Keep out without a qualified guide.

- These are big mountains, and they can never be totally swept by patrollers at the end of the day. A miniature electronic locator for your pocket is a cheap and effective safety precaution.

- If you want to keep tabs on your friends or kids, rent a few miniature pocket pagers during your visit. The system is efficient, and there are telephones at all of the mountain restaurants and warm-up huts.

WHERE TO STAY

The choice and variety of accommodation at Whistler is what sets the resort apart from almost all others. The options are as vast as the skiing, ranging from the ultra-luxurious and obscenely expensive to comfortable and affordable pensions and bed & breakfasts. Too numerous to list in their entirety, here are some personal favorites, based on the all-important cost criterion.

All rooms in Whistler can be booked through Whistler Central Reservations at (toll-free Canada & U.S.) 1-800-759-1015, FAX (604) 932-7231.

Here's a tip. Central Reservations is paid a commission of 10–20 percent for making your reservation, and that is included in the price quoted to you. You can save a few dollars by calling the toll-free number, getting a list of places that suit your needs, then making your own booking. Don't be afraid to haggle for at least a 10 percent discount.

There are three areas in the Whistler complex. Your choice depends on three factors: price, convenience and peace. The village, with all its activities, is the busiest and the noisiest. If you want to be near the action, but still be able to get a good night's sleep, ask for a room facing the slopes, away from the village. The Whistler Creek area, about 3 mi (5 km) from the village, is quieter. If you want to make use of village facilities, there is a regular and efficient shuttle bus service between the village and Whistler Creek. The Benchlands, at the base of Blackcomb, is also on the quiet side, but also expensive.

Expensive

Château Whistler Resort
The newest of the CP Hotel castles that dot ski country (see listings under Banff, Lake Louise and Quebec City), the Château Whistler has conceded nothing to its older cousins in style and opulence on the inside, although locals are less than enamored of its outside styling—they mockingly refer to it as "The Alpine General Hospital." Inside, its 343 rooms range from overly large bachelors to ultra-luxurious two-level suites with jacuzzi bath tubs, multiple TVs and original art. Located conveniently at the base of the Blackcomb lifts, the Château features an indoor/outdoor swimming pool, health club, hot tubs, dining rooms, lounges, a dozen designer shops and room rates to match. The low end of the scale is $160, and you can pay up to $850 a night for an executive suite, single or double occupancy (add $30 for each additional person).
4599 Chateau Blvd. Tel (604) 938-8000
Visa, MC, Amex, Diners, enRoute, Discover, JCB, T/CK

Delta Mountain Inn
In the heart of Whistler Village, a snowball's throw from the lifts, the Mountain Inn is the flagship of the Delta chain. Rooms are large and well appointed, and range from standard hotel rooms and studios with lofts to one-bedroom suites with fireplaces. Some suites have kitchens. Hotel facilities include dining rooms, fitness and health facilities and covered tennis courts.

Rates $85–$350 per night single or double occupancy.
4050 Whistler Way. Tel (604) 932-1982, toll-free (Canada) 1-800-268-1133, (U.S.) 1-800-877-1133
Visa, MC, Amex, Diners, enRoute, Discover, JCB, T/CK

Le Chamois

Small but luxurious, Le Chamois has 50 studios and one-bedroom suites, some with kitchens and jacuzzis. There are also a dozen three-bedroom executive suites accommodating up to eight people. Located at the Blackcomb Benchlands base, Le Chamois's ski-in/ski-out convenience comes at a price— room rates start at $140 and run up to $650. Ski weekends and packages are available.
4557 Blackcomb Way. Tel (604) 932-8700, toll-free 1-800-777-0185
Visa, MC, Amex, Diners, T/CK

Moderate

Hearthstone Lodge

Designed by Arthur Erickson, the stylish Hearthstone is small, with just 19 suites. Located in the heart of Whistler Village, it has one-, two- and three-bedroom units, most with kitchens and fireplaces, and it has a grocery market and liquor store on the premises. Rates $145–$475.
4211 Sunshine Place. Tel (604) 932-4161, toll-free (U.S. & Canada) 1-800-663-7711
Visa, MC, Amex

Lake Placid Lodge

At Whistler Creek, this lodge has 106 units, ranging from studios to three-bedrooms. Some are equipped with kitchen and fireplace. Also has pool, jacuzzi and sauna. Rates $69–$275.
2050 Lake Placid Rd. Tel (604) 932-6999
Visa, MC, Amex

Mountainside Lodge

Across the street from the Keg in the middle of the village, the Mountainside has a combination of 89 studios and studios with a loft. All units have kitchens

and a fireplace. Also has a pool, sauna and jacuzzi. Rates $85–$260 double or quad occupancy.
Sundial Place. Tel (604) 932-4511, toll-free (U.S. & Canada) 1-800-777-8135
Visa, MC, Amex, T/CK

Nancy Greene Lodge

Although Nancy and husband Al Raine no longer own the lodge, she can still be seen chatting to the guests, and her memorabilia from the glory days at the 1968 Olympics still adorn the lobby. This European-style hotel has 137 rooms, 40 of them suites with kitchens, balconies and fireplaces. Overall, the rooms are extremely small, but the hotel is centrally located and just steps from the lifts in the middle of the village. Good memories and pretty good value here. Rates $110–$170 double occupancy.
4154 Village Green. Tel (604) 932-2221, toll-free (U.S. & Canada) 1-800-667-3363
Visa, MC, Amex, Diners, enRoute, JCB, T/CK

Tantalus Lodge

Large two-bedroom units, all equipped with kitchen and a fireplace, are ideal for families or groups. Also has a heated outdoor pool, sauna and jacuzzi. Five minutes' walk from Whistler Village. In ski season the lodge runs a free shuttle to and from the lifts. Rates $185–$299 quad occupancy.
4200 Whistler Way. Tel (604) 932-4146, toll-free (Canada) 1-800-268-1133, (U.S.) 1-800-877-1133
Visa, MC, Amex, Diners, T/CK

Whistler Fairways Hotel

A large (194 rooms) resort hotel, the Fairways is in Whistler Village adjacent to the golf course. Ideal if you want to be centrally located, but away from the busy village center, it's still within an easy walk of the lifts. Rooms range from studios to one- and two-bedroom suites. Facilities include a heated outdoor pool and jacuzzi, sauna and a small gym. Rates $105–$450.
4005 Whistler Way. Tel (604) 932-2522, toll-free (U.S. & Canada) 1-800-663-5644
Visa, MC, Amex, Diners

Inexpensive

"Cheap accommodation" is almost an oxymoron in Whistler, but for the budget-minded pensions and bed & breakfast establishments are your best bet. None are right in the village, but most are no more than a mile or so away. For the price, the drive is a minor inconvenience.

Alta Vista Chalet
Eight units. Just over a mile (2 km) from village. Doubles $95–$119, breakfast and afternoon tea included.
3229 Archibald Way. Tel (604) 932-4900, FAX (604) 932-4933
Visa, MC, T/CK

Chalet Luise
Seven rooms in Swiss decor. Completely non-smoking. Whirlpool and sauna. Half a mile (1 km) from village. Doubles $85–$119, full breakfast included. Ski packages available.
7461 Ambassador Cres. Tel (604) 932-4187
Visa, MC, T/CK

Edelweiss Pension
Eight rooms, plus sauna and jacuzzi. Half a mile (1 km) from village. Doubles $89–$119, breakfast included.
7162 Nancy Greene Dr. Tel (604) 932-3641
Visa, MC, Amex, T/CK

Haus Heidi
Seven rooms, non-smoking. Also has jacuzzi and sauna. Situated in a quiet area a mile (1.6 km) from village. Doubles $89–$109, full breakfast included.
7115 Nester's Rd. Tel (604) 932-3113
Visa, MC, T/CK

UBC Lodge
Dormitory sleeping. Kitchen, games room, sauna and hot tub. Bedding required. $10–$20 per person per night.
2124 Nordic Dr. Tel (604) 932-6604, or book by credit card through UBC Student Union Bldg, (604) 822-5851
Cash, T/CK only at Lodge

Whistler Youth Hostel
Dormitory sleeping only, has do-it-yourself kitchen, sauna, games room and fireplace lounge. Bedding can be rented or bring your own. $10–$17.50 per person per night.
5678 Alta Lake Rd. Tel (604) 932-5492
Visa, MC, T/CK

HOTELS vs CONDOS vs CHALETS

There's nothing if not variety in accommodation at Whistler, and besides the usual hotel facilities, there are condominium units and individual chalets. At one time the distinction between hotel rooms and condos was that condos had kitchen facilities so you could prepare your own meals. That's less so these days with many hotel suites containing kitchens. Perhaps the one distinction that remains is price. For the most part, condo units, minus amenities such as doormen, valets, room service and other perks, are cheaper. Likewise for individual chalets and cabins, which also can be found away from the hub-bub of the village, in one of the various residential areas or on the slopes of Whistler and Blackcomb. Families and large groups often prefer chalets and cabins for their cook-at-home convenience and for having a little more space and solitude. Here's a list of companies that can help you book everything from a cabin in the woods to a four-bedroom condo with hot tub and sauna.

Crown Resort Accommodations
Crown Resort lists over 50 luxury townhouses and condos, ranging in size from one to four bedrooms. All are within skiing distance of the lifts, and most come with fireplaces, hot tubs and great views. Rates $65–$500 double occupancy.
Box 1018, Whistler, B.C. V0N 1B0. Tel (604) 932-2215
Visa, MC

Rainbow Retreats
This company specializes in single-family homes, duplexes and townhouses ranging in size from one to five bedrooms. Various locations are available, including ski-in/ski-out proximity to the lifts. Some properties also feature hot tubs and saunas. Rates $75–$600 depending on number of bedrooms and guests.
2129 Lake Placid Rd. Tel (604) 932-2343, FAX (604) 932-2969
Visa, MC, Amex, Diners, T/CK

Whiski Jack Resorts
Has seven condominium properties in Whistler Village and the valley. Units range from studio to four-bedroom, with the option of fireplaces, VCRs, pools, hot tubs and indoor tennis. Rates $85–$550 depending on unit.
Box 344, Whistler, B.C. V0N 1B0. Tel (604) 932-6500
Visa, MC, Amex

Whistler Chalets & Accommodations
Has over 100 individual properties in Whistler Village and resort (with ski-in/ski-out locations), and on Blackcomb and Whistler Cay Heights, ranging from one- to four-bedroom condos to private homes. Rates $49–$700 depending on property and number of people.
Box 747, Whistler, B.C. V0N 1B0. Tel (604) 932-6699; toll-free (U.S. & Canada) 1-800-663-7711
Visa MC, Amex

WHERE TO EAT
When it comes to lunch on the slopes, there is a big difference between Whistler and Blackcomb.

Whistler
The mountain has three places to chow down, and all three are basic, crowded and expensive. On a sunny day they're wonderful places to soak up the sun and enjoy your own knapsack lunch. I prefer to ski to the village or Whistler Creek.

Mid-station
At the base of the Redline Quad. Small, limited sandwich fare, and expensive. However, a good place to take your own lunch to enjoy without the crowds.

Pika's At Roundhouse Station
Basic burgers and fast food with slow lineups.

The Roundhouse
Walk up the extra 50 feet from Pika's—it's worth it. Salads, pizza, roast beef on a bun. Less crowded and better food than Pika's.

Blackcomb

Blackcomb has made an art form out of on-mountain eating.

Christine's in the Rendezvous
Gourmet dining a mile in the sky, Christine's is all white linen and crystal. Try the beef tenderloin or the chicken Yudan. On a sunny day, book a table at Christine's Bistro outdoors on the deck. Reservation a must: 932-2775.

Crystal Hut
A cozy log cabin with a wonderful view of the mountains and the valley. A great place to avoid the lunch-hour crush at the Rendezvous. Perfect on a sunny day. Try the buffalo burgers.

Horstman Hut
At the top of the Seventh Heaven Chair, this has to be one of the most scenic eateries anywhere. Provides a Bavarian lunch for under $10, and the million-dollar view is free. You can also pack a knapsack and picnic with the gods.

A few tips on lunch:
- *The busiest time at any of the on-mountain restaurants is between 12 and 2.*
- *Take your own. Both mountains are friendly to the brown bag set, so put it in a knapsack, and take along a small cable or ski lock so you can secure it to a tree at the summit. You won't be alone: you'll see hundreds of knapsacks decorating the shrubbery.*
- *If you're in a hurry, try the Ski-Inns in various locations on Whistler. Without stepping out of your boards you can grab a hot drink and barbecue your own dog or burger on the nearby grills.*
- *You could skip lunch altogether by having brunch at the Château Whistler. It's the best in town and will carry you over to the dinner hour.*

And here are my recommendations for dinner:

Expensive

Araxis
A combination of Italian and French dishes including fresh seafood, homemade pasta and fresh game all done in a northern Mediterranean style. Reservations recommended.
In Village Square. Tel 932-4540
Visa, MC, Amex

Chez Joel
Features fondues of all flavors and a legendary veal schnitzel. Also try the Sunday afternoon raclette. Reservations recommended.
In Village Square. Tel 932-2112
Visa, MC, Amex, T/CK

Hatto's Deli
A pricey little deli located in the St. Andrew's House in the village, Hatto's has all the traditional deli sandwiches, pasta salads and high-end yuppie snack food. Tel 932-8345. Next door is the Cookie Company (932-2962), with the best cookies in Whistler—great homemade monster cookies with a variety of exotic fillings.

Les Deux Gros
Located just south of the village down by the Creekside, Les Deux Gros features French cuisine with an emphasis on spirited sauces and fresh game. Reservations recommended.
1200 Alta Lake Rd. Tel 932-4611
Visa, MC, Amex

Rimrock Café & Oyster Bar
Trendy and sophisticated, the Rimrock is the dining spot to be seen in, and gets my vote as the best restaurant in town. The oysters are superb, as are the specialty seafood dishes. Reservations definitely recommended. Down at the Creekside.
2001 Whistler Rd. Tel 932-5565
Visa, MC, Amex

Sushi Village
West coast fresh fish—sushi or sashimi, plus teriyaki and other traditional Japanese dishes. A fun place that's great for large groups. Saki served in quart bottles. Reservations for groups recommended.
In the Westbrook Hotel, 4272 Mountain Square. Tel 932-3330
Visa, MC, Amex, Diners, JCB

Umberto's
Primo Italian food at any one of three locations: the original Umberto's in the

village, the Trattoria in the Mountainside Lodge, and Fetabello's in the Whistler Creek Lodge. Reservations recommended. Tel 932-4442 (Village), 932-5858 (Mountainside) or 932-3000 (Whistler Creek)
Visa, MC, Diners, enRoute, CB, JCB

Moderate

La Fiesta
Something a little different—a Spanish tapas bar. Good value, and a good place for groups.
In the Château Whistler, 4599 Chateau Blvd. Tel 938-2040
Visa, MC, Amex, Diners, enRoute

Monk's Grill
Prime rib is the specialty. Casual atmosphere, with stone fireplace. Has a kid's menu before 6:30 p.m. The bar serves burgers and pizza and has a big-screen TV. Free parking in the Glacier Lodge after 5.
At the base of Blackcomb, next to the Château Whistler. Tel 932-9677
Visa, MC, Amex, enRoute

Twigs
Twigs is your typical hotel dining room, but it is a safe and reliable bet with a menu that covers the full range.
In the Delta Mountain Inn, 4050 Whistler Way. Tel 932-1982
Visa, MC, Amex

Wainwright's
Classic Canadian fare, nothing fancy, including the prices. Nice atmosphere.
In Nancy Greene Lodge, 4154 Village Green. Tel 938-1921
Visa, MC, Amex

Inexpensive

Café Presto
A small deli opposite McConkey's in the village, it's a great place to grab your early morning coffee and muffin to take up the mountain. Also has good lunch and dinnertime snacks.
Beside the Whistler gondola. Tel 932-6009

Hoz's Pub
Down at the Creekside, Hoz's is frequented by locals looking for good basic burger and chicken fare. A good selection of appetizers that you can make a meal out of.
Tel 932-5940
Visa, MC, Amex

The Keg
A popular choice with locals, the Keg has basic pub grub, plus some mainstream items that won't break your budget. Great salad bar. Can get crowded at times, but the service is fast, and the location in the village is convenient. Get there before 6 or after 10 if you don't want to line up. No reservations.
In Sundial Place. Tel 932-5151
Visa, MC, Amex, Diners, enRoute

Misty Mountain Pizza
The best pizza in Whistler, with eat-in, take-out or delivery service. Serves by the slice, and is a great late-night haunt for those with an après-ski, après-drinking appetite.
In the Royal Bank building behind the Conference Centre. Tel 932-2825
No cards

Moguls
With the best muffins and coffee in Whistler, it's a great spot for breakfast. Everything is homemade, and the coffee is Starbucks, all the rage among the coffee cognoscenti on the West Coast.
In the village, adjacent to the pharmacy. Tel 932-4845
No cards

Peter's Underground
Right in the middle of the village, a great place to drop in on your way to the lifts in the morning for muffins, health cookies and excellent coffee. Also serves lunch and dinner, including a great pizza.
4115 Golfer's Approach. Tel 932-4811
Visa, MC, Amex

South Side Deli and Diner
The deli is great for eat-in or take-out. Good prices, good selection of deli treats, and a good place to pick up early morning tips from the locals. Down at the Creekside end of Lake Placid Rd. Tel 932-3368
Visa

NIGHTLIFE

There's no doubt about it, Whistler is a happening place when it comes to nightlife. You can dance up a storm, boogie till the wee hours, sip cocktails at a piano bar, swap tales in a jock bar or just sit back and watch the live entertainment—if you have the energy after a day's skiing.

Right After Skiing
Head for either the *Longhorn* at the bottom of Whistler or *Merlin's* up at the Benchlands. Both are loud, happening places with huge sundecks, great music and a crowd just beaming from the day's skiing and aching for action.

Loud and Lively
Buffalo Bill's
This is Whistler's live band emporium, featuring everything from rock-and-roll relics to groups just a touch outside the mainstream. Good vibes and good dancing, and a two-tiered bar. Look out for hefty cover charges up to $20, depending on the entertainment. And don't bother getting there before 10.
In the Timberline Lodge, across from Conference Centre. Tel 932-5211

The Savage Beagle
A mainstay of the Whistler dance set, the Beagle starts to rock right after skiing and continues with loud music, savage shooters, blinding light shows and cheek to jowl crowds.
In Village Square. Tel 932-4540

Tommy Africa's Club
A taste of the avant-garde, this is Whistler's hottest new dance club. The music rocks, the crowd is oh so trendy, the light show dazzles and the lineups are long. Doesn't really get rolling until after 10.
In the Blackcomb Lodge, 4220 Gateway Dr. Tel 932-6090

WHISTLER—
FIVE 5-STAR FAVORITES

Best Run for Vertical
Olympic Run

Best Overall Run
Franz's

Best Restaurant
Sushi Village

Best Nightclub/Bar
Buffalo Bill's

Best Accommodation
Château Whistler
  John Colpitts, Whistler

BLACKCOMB—
FIVE 5-STAR FAVORITES

Best Run for Vertical
Whistler Bowl

Best Overall Run
Whistler Cirque

Best Restaurant
Rimrock Café & Oyster Bar

Best Nightclub/Bar
Savage Beagle

Best Accommodation
Delta Mountain Inn
  Paul Morrison, Whistler

For the Brew Crew

The Boot Pub

The Boot is a Whistler institution that has been around since the first lift was installed. Definitely a down-home draft-drinking place, with diversions such as darts, pool and occasionally live entertainment.
Next to the Shoestring Lodge, 7124 Nancy Greene Dr. Tel 932-3338

Jimmy D's

Whistler's version of an old-style American roadhouse featuring old-gold rock, large-screen TVs, pinball machines and a ping pong table. Very casual, very basic.
4005 Whistler Way Rd. Tel 932-2522

Longhorn Pub

The Longhorn is especially popular right at the end of skiing—especially if it's sunny, when the monster deck is perfect for catching the day's last rays. Later on it's still pretty busy—some folks don't bother leaving—when the live entertainment starts. Also has pool tables.
In the Carleton Lodge, at the bottom of the Whistler Express. Tel 932-5999

Tapley's Pub

A more traditional drinking spot, with the emphasis on beer, beer and more beer. Also has darts, shuffleboard and plenty of sports on numerous TV screens.
4068 Golfer's Approach, across from Conference Centre. Tel 932-4011

Mellow

Mallard Bar

Sedate and serene, the Mallard is dressy with a mood to match the style of the Château. If you want style and sophistication, this is your nightcap stop. In the Château Whistler, 4599 Chateau Blvd. Tel 938-8000

Nancy's Lounge

Mellow is the right word. A place for the after-dinner crowd to sip cognac and listen to live jazz and blues. You might even meet Nancy. In Nancy Greene Lodge, 4154 Village Green. Tel 932-2221

DIVERSIONS

Games and Movies

Whistler Wonderland, a games arcade in the Conference Centre, has 40 or so of the latest electronic toys, plus miniature golf. In the same building is the Rainbow Theatre with two showings nightly. First-run movies are changed weekly. It's a great place to unload the kids. For video rentals, check out Boyd's Videos, just outside the village at Nester's shopping plaza.

Heli-Skiing

Every skier has to do it once! Whistler and Blackcomb have the advantage of providing heli-skiing on any one of a half-dozen nearby glaciers for a day, or even half a day. Most of it is on terrain that is manageable for advanced intermediates. The tab is about $300 for four of the most spectacular runs you'll ever take.

Who's Minding the Kids?

Both mountains have programs that take kids aged 2 to 12. Whistler has Ski Scamps, with three age groups: 2–2, 3–6 and 7–12. Scampland is halfway up at the Olympic station and is for ages 2–12. Over on Blackcomb, Wee Wizards take 2-to-3-year-olds, and 4-to-12-year-olds head for Super Kids.

Activities in these programs include morning ski lessons, crafts, story telling and for the young ones that all-important afternoon nap. For info call Whistler's Ski Scamp programs at 932-3434; or Blackcomb's Kid's Kamps at 932-3141.

Police Emergency 932-3044

Ski Finders 932-3111

Whistler Medical Centre
932-4911

Whistler Office Services
932-5114

Whistler Resort Association
932-4222

Whistler Rental
Accommodation 932-6500

Ski Shops —
McConkey's 932-2391
Whistler Bootfit Shop
932-9669
Precision Ski 932-4899
Can Ski 932-1975

Air B.C. 1-800-663-0522

Air Canada 1-800-663-3721

Canadian Airlines 932-5551

Maverick Coach Lines
in Whistler 932-5031

Perimeter Transportation
1-800-663-4265 from
Whistler

B.C. Rail 932-4003 for local
information

Whistler Taxi 932-5455

Sea to Sky Taxi 932-8294

Budget Car Rental 932-1236

Husky Towing 938-1300

Harold's Towing 932-3416

Blackcomb Catering

For that special occasion, or when you just don't feel like whipping up a meal for your closest traveling companions, give yourself a break and call Blackcomb Catering. From intimate gourmet meals in the comfort of your own condo or chalet to a salmon BBQ (fresh B.C. salmon, naturally) on the top of Blackcomb—the menu is limited only by your imagination and appetite. Call 932-4717.

Ski Rentals and Boot Fitting

There are many ski shops in Whistler, but Jim McConkey's in the Village Square (and three other locations) is a cut above most. Although until recently it was the place for the gold-card set to pick up nifty $3,000 ski suits, now its priority is on rentals, repairs and accessories. If you're thinking of buying skis and want to demo some high-end models, it's the place to go. There's always a good selection of meticulously tuned race or performance skis on hand. If you're having trouble with your boots, ask for John Colpitts; he's one of Canada's best boot-fitting experts, and his sure hands can cure almost any problem with fit.

Your other choice is The Whistler Bootfit Shop. Ask for Dave Steers. Don't try anybody else (except John at McConkey's). Dave can cure all those pinches, pains and sloppy performance problems for about $25. Located in Delta Mountain Inn. Call 932-9669.

Lost Skis

If you lose a ski on the slopes, don't panic, help is at hand in the form of Ski Finders. These ski seekers roam the mountain with metal detectors strapped to their backs, and have a 90 percent success rate in finding lost equipment. For a flat fee of $100 they'll spend up to two hours looking for your lost ski. A couple of tips from owner Eric White: mark the spot where you fell, and give them other details such as which way you were turning, how far you fell and how much speed you were carrying. Call 932-3111.

Ski Esprit

It is said the average skier could holiday at Whistler and Blackcomb for five years and never entirely discover the mountains. The "Ski Esprit" instruction and guide program is therefore a terrific introduction to both mountains and just a fun way to meet people and spend a few days with an instructor. The program is not heavy on instruction. Mainly it's just skiing and having some laughs during the day and at après-ski functions. The tab is about $125 for three days.

The Ski Esprit folks host an information and social gathering at 6:30 p.m. every Thursday and Sunday in the Conference Centre. This excellent introduction to the mountains and facilities is open to everyone, even if you have no intention of signing up for the program. Call 932-3928.

All Seasons Sports Massage

The hot tub works wonders after a tough day on the slopes, but if that doesn't get out all the kinks, put yourself in the good hands of Sandra Rathwell or Colleen Fraser-White. Together they run All Seasons Sports Massage at the Château Whistler, Delta Mountain Inn and in the St. Andrew's House. Let their fingers do the walking all over your aching body—$60 for an hour, $35 a half-hour—and you'll be ready for action the next day. They'll even come to your hotel room. Call 938-1555, or 932-7336 to book.

Whistler Brewery

Whistler has almost everything else, so why not its own brewery? The Whistler Brewing Company produces two commendable brews, Whistler Lager and Black Tusk Ale, that sold the equivalent of 1,000,000 bottles in Whistler alone last year, and attract fans across B.C. If you feel like seeing the brewmasters at work, tours of the brewery are run every afternoon throughout the winter. Naturally, sampling is part of the tour. The Whistler Brewery is at Function Junction, about 6 mi (10 km) south of the village. Call 932-6185.

THE OKANAGAN VALLEY

HOW TO GET THERE

By Plane: All the resorts in the Okanagan Valley are accessible from Kelowna Airport. Canadian Airlines has daily flights from Vancouver and Calgary, with connections from most major centers.

By Car: From Vancouver it's about a four-hour drive along the Coquihalla Highway. From Calgary, Vernon is about five hours along Trans-Canada 1 through Banff, Lake Louise and Golden, then through Rogers Pass and into Revelstoke. About 30 mi (48 km) west of Revelstoke, take Hwy 97A south into Vernon.

By Bus: Greyhound Bus Lines runs daily trips into the Okanagan from Vancouver, Calgary and Edmonton.

Like so many other places on the Canadian ski map, B.C.'s fruit-growing Okanagan Valley is more renowned for its summertime tourism appeal than its winter attractions. Still, plenty of people come to enjoy the ski resorts of the region and the crispest, lightest, most reliable snow in the province.

The resorts of the Okanagan are studies in contrast, but they do share several features. They are, for the most part, still uncrowded, compared to Whistler or Banff. The weather is remarkably predictable—neither too wet nor too cold—and the sunny skies are not just the brochure-speak of zealous marketers.

Then there's the snow—lots of it. Although the valley remains mostly snow-free throughout the winter, the resorts sit high above on peaks blessed with a light, dry powder.

Many skiers are eschewing the crowds, cost and unpredictable weather of Whistler to ski the Okanagan. Not so many, though, that the slopes are absurdly crowded. There's lots of room in the Okanagan, and lengthy lift lines are rare.

This is a region where a car is your best friend. Theoretically, it is possible to ski all four Okanagan resorts in one week, but with recent development each resort could easily satisfy you for a full week. However, it would be a mistake to not ski at least two if you're in the region for more than a few days. And the driving is easy. The low-lying Okanagan Valley is virtually snow-free—by mid-February the golf courses are starting to open—and it's not until the final 10 or 20 minutes of driving that you encounter any snow.

The annual average of about 300 in (760 cm) is not as prodigious as in the Coastals or to the northeast in the Kootenays, but it arrives early and stays late, making spring skiing in the Okanagan a sun-kissed touch of bliss. And yes, it's true, you can ski and play golf in the same day.

The other lure of the Okanagan is the network of communities that offer an alternative to on-site villages. These are real towns, not insta-ski communities. They have roots, people like you and me, and a muffler shop or a burger joint or banks and post offices.

The skiing, though, is still what you come for. And if you happen to share a slice of life in Vernon, Penticton, Kelowna or Kamloops, that's also part of the Okanagan flavor.

For my money, the two best resorts in the region are Silver Star and Big White.

SILVER STAR MOUNTAIN RESORT

Box 2
Silver Star Mountain, B.C.
V0E 1G0
Tel (604) 542-0224

HOW TO GET THERE

By Plane: Kelowna Airport has connecting flights from Calgary and other major centers. The Silver Star free shuttle service meets all incoming flights to take you up to the resort.

By Car: From Vancouver, it's an easy and scenic four-hour drive along the Coquihalla Highway. From Calgary follow Trans-Canada 1 west to Sicamous and then take Hwy 97 south into Vernon. It's about 6 1/2 hours' drive.

By Bus: Regular bus service is available from Vancouver and Calgary via Greyhound Bus Lines.

A lot has happened at Silver Star in the past year. First of all it doubled in size, making it the second-largest resort in B.C. The development of the new Putnam Creek area also increased its vertical to 2,500 (762 m), giving it the biggest in the Okanagan. And to service 23 new runs, the longest high-speed quad chairlift in Canada was installed. That would be impressive enough, but it's really just the icing on the cake for this first-rate resort, which over the past five years has become one of the best ski areas in western Canada.

Located 14 mi (22 km) from the city of Vernon, Silver Star Village is a superbly designed resort, with architecture modeled on the 1890s Victorian gaslight era. Strict design guidelines and careful development have produced an impressive collection of hotels, private chalets, restaurants, lounges and other facilities with a distinctive old-west flavor.

Silver Star is nestled on the southern face of Aberdeen Mountain and provides ski-in/ski-out convenience for guests and a picturesque stroll-about environment perfectly in tune with the surrounding peaks of the Monashee Mountains. It's the self-contained convenience that made Silver Star an ideal destination for families, yet now the opening of the north-side slopes makes it a desirable destination for anyone looking for a big-mountain western experience.

THE SKIING

For the longest time, despite some excellent skiing, the biggest knock against Silver Star was its lack of vertical and the lack of expert skiing. That all changed in 1992 with the opening of the Putnam Creek Basin on the north side of Silver Star Mountain. The addition of the 23 new trails increased by 150 percent the total skiable terrain,

Base Elevation:
3,780 ft (1150 m)

Summit Elevation:
6,280 ft (1915 m)

Vertical Drop:
2,500 ft (760 m)

Skiable Terrain:
850 acres (340 ha)

Number of Trails: 69

Longest Run: 5.2 mi (8.3 km)

Lifts & Capacity: 3 quads,
2 doubles, 3 surface lifts;
4,800 skiers per hour

Daily Lift Ticket: $35
Weekly: $150

Annual Snowfall:
200 in (500 cm)

No. Days Skiing 91–92: 143

Snowmaking: None

Terrain Mix:
N 15%, I 55%, E 30%

Snow Phone: 542-1745

giving Silver Star 850 acres (340 ha), with light-dry powder that arrives early and stays late. Dubbed the "Valley of Adventure," 90 percent of the new terrain is designated as advanced or expert, although a 5-mi (8-km) easy cruising novice trail will give everyone a chance to check out the new development.

The 69 runs on both sides of the mountain are a near perfect blend of the tough and the tame, and the combination of two quad chairs, two doubles and a surface lift give efficient access to all terrain. And most of that terrain is below the treeline, which makes it comfortable to ski virtually anywhere on the mountain, even when the normally reliable Okanagan sun doesn't shine.

The snow is reliable also, with an annual average of 200 in (500 cm) providing plenty of opportunity to find untracked powder, particularly on the northwest face, where the secluded bus runs are found, and on the north face, where the new trails of the Putnam Creek area were cut.

Most of the intermediate runs are found via the summit chair on the southeast side, where a slew of long cruisers, such as Big Dipper and Exhibition, and a pair of mogul chutes, like Little Dipper and Middle Dipper, provide some heads-up action. Farther to the southeast are a pair of long novice runs that carry you safely back to the village.

Most of the serious skiing is found on the bus runs (so-called because a bus takes you back to the base after each run) and in the Putnam Creek area. The bus runs are a particular favorite because they are isolated. They start above the treeline and finish deep in the forest, without a lift tower or lineup in sight. On the backside the pull of the 2,500 vertical ft (760 m) is best experienced on runs like Holy Smokes, GowaBunga and Headwall, but if you just want some giant slalom cruising, try a combination of Bergerstrasse, Aunt Gladys and Sunny Ridge.

It's that kind of variety that has vaulted Silver Star into the big leagues of western skiing. Yet it has achieved that without many of the costly trappings and pell-mell development that plague other resorts.

HOW TO SKI SILVER STAR

Novices

You can connect to beginner runs from any of the lifts, but try the Grand Tour. Take the Town T-bar to Mid T-bar to Silver Queen Quad. Take the long easy cruise down to the base of Vance Creek Express and take Bergerstrasse to the bottom of Putnam Creek Express. From there take Main Street Skiway back down to the village. A total of 9.5 mi (15 km), it all takes about 2 1/2 hours.

Intermediates

Take Town T-bar to Mid T-bar and take Skunk Hollow or Blast Off down to the base of Vance Creek Express. Try a couple of good long cruising runs on either Big Dipper or Whisky Jack. Now you're ready to head for the Putnam Creek Side. Take Vance Creek Quad back to summit, and take Eureka to Sunny Ridge. From top of Putnam Creek Express take Bergerstrasse to the short but steep chutes of Gypsy Queen, Caliper Ridge or, for a real snowy challenge, the GowaBunga Bowl.

Experts

Take Town T-bar to Mid T-bar, then play around in the steep, deep snow runs of the Attridge Face. Try Bus Back and Fast Back for some reliable powder, but just remember you have to be shuttled back to the village. When you're warmed up, head over to the Putnam Creek side, to try Sunny Glades, Back Bowl, Headwall and GowaBunga Bowl.

WHERE TO STAY

Although Vernon is only 14 mi (22 km) down the road from the Silver Star base village, most visitors prefer to stay on-site because of the ski-to-your-door convenience. There's a good variety of accommodations to choose from, and all are moderately priced.

You can book accommodation through Silver Star Central Reservations, at (604) 542-0224, toll-free (Sept to April) 1-800-663-4431.

Moderate

The Kickwillie Inn and the Pinnacles
If it's space and privacy you want, these two apartment complexes are your best choice. The Kickwillie has seven one- and two-bedroom family suites with bedroom, dining room, living room and kitchen. (Ask for one with a fireplace.) Rates $105–$185 per unit. The Pinnacles has 16 deluxe large suites, with two, three or four bedrooms. Rates $175–$385 per unit. Amenities in each suite include a kitchen, private sundeck, rooftop hot tub and fireplace. Ideal for two families. Tel (604) 542-4548
Visa, MC, Amex, T/CK

Lord Aberdeen Apartment Hotel
A little different than the hotel accommodation, with 16 one- and two-bedroom apartments. Each has a living room, bedroom and fully equipped kitchen. Rates $110–$190 per unit. Tel (604) 542-1992
Visa, MC, T/CK

Putnam Station Inn
A full-service hotel with 22 hotel-style rooms, plus eight one-bedroom suites with kitchens. All rooms and suites have TVs, plus there are outdoor hot tubs and a dining room. Rates $70–$90 double occupancy. Tel (604) 542-2459
Visa, MC, Amex, T/CK

Silver Lode Inn
All 21 rooms—four with kitchens—have either two double beds or one double plus a bunk bed. Also has hot tub and a lounge. Rates $70–$150 double occupancy. Tel (604) 549-5105
Visa, MC, Amex, T/CK

Vance Creek Hotel
The resort's flagship hotel, the Vance Creek has 51 luxury rooms—12 with kitchens—that sleep from four to six people. Amenities include a sauna, rooftop hot tubs and a Victorian-style dining room. Rates $80–$124 double occupancy. Tel (604) 549-5191
Visa, MC, Amex, T/CK

Thirty private residences are for rent in the Silver Star residential area called the Knoll. Designed in the same gaslight-era motif as the rest of the resort, they have ski-to-your-door access, and range in size from two to four bedrooms. I highly recommend these for families traveling together. Rates $225–$350 per unit. Book through Silver Star Central Reservations, (604) 542-0224

Visa, MC, Amex, T/CK

In Vernon

For those anxious to sample the delights of downtown Vernon, here are two favorites I recommend.

Moderate

Village Green Inn

Located right at the bottom of the Silver Star Rd, this is a large, rambling, post-Cuban-Missile-Crisis-styled hotel with 138 fairly large and comfortable rooms. Has a dining room, lounge and indoor pool. Ski packages are available. Rates average $80 double occupancy.

4801 27th St. Tel (604) 542-3321, toll-free (western Canada) 1-800-663-4433

Visa, MC, Amex, Diners, enRoute, JCB, T/CK

Vernon Lodge

A fairly large and rambling hotel with 131 good-sized rooms, some facing the indoor pool and tropical courtyard. Also has a dining room and bar. Rates $69 double occupancy.

3914 32nd St. Tel (604) 545-3385

Visa, MC, Amex, Diners, enRoute, Discover, T/CK

WHERE TO EAT

Moderate

Craigellachie Dining Room

The family dining room at Silver Star, with a good varied menu and great atmosphere. The decor is all early railroad. A comfortable place that feels like home.

In Putnam Station Inn, 147 Main St. Tel 542-2459

Visa, MC, Amex

SILVER STAR—
FIVE 5-STAR FAVORITES

Best Run for Vertical
GowaBunga

Best Overall Run
Bergerstrasse

Best Restaurant
Silver Lode Dining Room

Best Nightclub/Bar
Vance Creek Saloon

Best Accommodation
Kickwillie Inn
Mike Duggan, Silver Star

Silver Lode Dining Room
Specializes in traditional European dining, including raclette, fondue, bratwurst and veal. Swiss motif and atmosphere. A good place for couples. Reservations recommended.
In Silver Lode Inn. Tel 549-5105
Visa, MC, Amex

Vance Creek Dining Room
The most elegant dining room on the mountain, with a Victorian decor. A good selection of traditional Canadian dishes, along with some continental cuisine. Check out the daily specials. Sometimes has live entertainment. Reservations recommended during peak periods.
In the Vance Creek Hotel. Tel 549-5191
Visa, MC, Amex

In Vernon
Moderate
Café Campeache
A new spot in town, this trendy and colorful café serves a refreshing change from the more stolid fare found elsewhere. Call it hearty, home-cooked nouvelle cuisine. Almost everything from the herb bread to the French onion soup is made on the premises, and the entrees are an interesting mix of the traditional and the unusual. Try the pork tenderloin with mustard or the chicken breast with mushrooms and brandy.
3202 31st Ave. Tel 542-1518
Visa, MC, Amex, T/CK

Earl's
Funky and fun, Earl's features a Californian menu with an emphasis on tasty lean cuisine items such as stir-frys and various chicken dishes. Great

atmosphere.
In Fruit Union Square. Tel 542-3370
Visa, MC, Amex, T/CK

Intermezzo
This friendly owner-operated restaurant is one of my favorites in the Okanagan. It has a Mediterranean menu heavy on veal and pasta, with some interesting twists. Good service.
3206 34th Ave. Tel 542-3853
Visa, MC, Amex, T/CK

NIGHTLIFE
Loud and Lively
Vance Creek Saloon
A large and raucous après-ski gathering spot where the action continues well into the evening with live bands and a cowboy-mining-old-time-music-hall atmosphere. Theme nights are common, along with old-time fiddle shows and serious dancing.
In the Vance Creek Hotel. Tel 549-5191

Mellow
Okanagan Wine Cellar
The Wine Cellar is a great place for a couple to toddle off to for some quiet fireside contemplation and sipping. Its specialty is the many wines produced in the Okanagan, along with some local beers. Just right for those quieter moments.
In the Putnam Station Inn, 147 Main St. Tel 542-2459

In Vernon
Alexander's
A good neighborhood pub, with a slightly loud crowd, plus some games including darts. A lively place, especially on Thursday nights, when wings are the drawing card.
12408 Kalamalka, on Kalamalka Lake. Tel 545-3131

Squire's Four
A great little neighborhood pub done up in Tudor style, with lots of wood and

SILVER STAR—USEFUL TELEPHONE NUMBERS
(area code 604)

Medical Centre 545-5321

Chamber of Commerce
545-0771

Golf Courses:
Predator Ridge 542-3436
Spallumcheen 545-5824

Vernon Airporter (Airport &
Mountain) 545-0527

Greyhound Bus Lines
545-0527

Avis 1-800-879-2847

Hertz 765-3822

brass. A healthy dose of atmosphere and a good selection of imported beers.
On Stickle Rd, 1 mi (1.5 km) north of Village Green Hotel on Hwy 97. Tel 549-2144

DIVERSIONS

Silver Star's Nordic Centre

With more and more families dividing up between the alpine and cross-country side of things, the Silver Star Nordic Centre is a definite bonus. It's an impressive trail system that has hosted numerous Nordic World Cup Competitions and is the official training facility for the Canadian cross-country and biathlon ski teams. There are 15.5 mi (25 km) of trails, plus waxing facilities, rentals and instruction; nearly 2 mi (3 km) are lit for night skiing. Nearby Silver Star Provincial Park has an additional 50 mi (80 km) of trails. Call 542-0224.

In the Swim

Although all accommodation at Silver Star has hot tubs, the Aquatic Centre is still a great diversion for water sports. It has a 25-by-50-foot pool, hot tubs, change rooms and a laundry. It's a perfect place to unwind after a day on the slopes. Call 542-0224.

A Touch of the Grape

The resort goes to great lengths to capitalize on the region's second-biggest asset—after the skiing—by promoting and presenting the local wines. For oenophiles it's a great opportunity to please your palate with a selection from more than 15 vineyards. You'll find an extensive selection in all the restaurants, though serious sippers will find the largest selection at the Okanagan Wine Cellar.

For those too timid to make their own decisions, here are a few recommendations: Mission Hill 1989

Chardonnay Bin 33, Gray Monk 1989 Chardonnay, Gray Monk 1991 Pinot Gris.

Golf & Ski Spree

And you thought Vancouver was the only place where you could ski and golf in the same day. Not true! Once the golf courses in the valley open in mid-March, anyone buying a full-price lift ticket can ski for the morning then head down to play a round at any one of the local courses. All for the price of your skiing. Ask at the Silver Star Mountain Resort ticket office, 542-0224.

BIG WHITE

Box 2039
Kelowna, B.C.
V1X 4K5
Tel (604) 765-3101

HOW TO GET THERE

By Plane: Big White is 34 mi (55 km) east of Kelowna Airport, which has regular connections from Calgary, Vancouver and other major centers.

By Car: From Vancouver, take the Coquihalla Highway; it's about a four-hour drive. From Calgary, take Trans-Canada 1 west to Hwy 97, then south into Kelowna; the drive is about 400 mi (650 km).

By Bus: Greyhound Bus Lines runs regular service from Calgary, Vancouver and other western cities. There's a free shuttle service from downtown Kelowna up to the mountain.

Big White is the highest resort village in B.C., and as you might guess about a ski area nestled above the treeline in the heart of the snow-rich Monashee Mountains, white stuff is what defines the resort's character. An average of 225 in (565 cm) a year falls on the resort.

The moment you alight from your car at the base area you are engulfed in a high-alpine world of blinding white light. You'll be dazzled by the high bowls, the sheer other-world whiteness of the 1,000 acres (400 ha) of open-face mountain skiing, and the vastness of the vista that rolls in great white waves away to the horizon. You'll often hear cynics refer to the resort as "Big Whiteout," and it's true, there are days when the fog is so thick that you can't see your pole plant. But there are also those days when the sky is so clear you can almost see the Pacific, for, like the rest of the Okanagan, Big White gets its share of brilliant sunny days.

At the center of all this is the sprawling terraced village development of Big White. It's a living, breathing self-contained community that under the serene white coating of winter hums with activity. There are hotels, plus a veritable village of 15 condominiums and numerous chalets with capacity for 3,300 skiers—all with ski-in/ski-out convenience. There are restaurants, bars, shops, saunas, hot tubs, a swimming pool, racquetball courts, a liquor store and, amazingly enough, underground parking.

It's more than enough to keep any skier happy for a week, and indeed many choose to do just that despite the proximity of other resorts. And nobody would question them—especially families, where the self-contained village provides daycare and baby-sitting, along with the peace of mind that comes from knowing everything you'll ever need for a week of skiing is right outside your door.

BIG WHITE—
STATISTICALLY SPEAKING

Base Elevation:
5,450 ft (1660 m)

Summit Elevation:
7,606 ft (2318 m)

Vertical Drop:
2,050 ft (625 m)

Skiable Terrain:
1,000 acres (400 ha)

Number of Trails: 51

Longest Run: 3.1 mi (5 km)

Lifts & Capacity: 3 quads,
1 triple, 1 double, 3 surface
lifts; 12,900 skiers per hour

Daily Lift Ticket: $36
Weekly: $165 (5 days)

Annual Snowfall:
225 in (565 cm)

No Days Skiing 91–92: 150

Snowmaking: None

Terrain Mix:
N 32%, I 41%, E 27%

Snow Phone: 765-SNOW

THE SKIING

Across the broad sprawling slice of the Monashees that Big White occupies, it's possible to find just about any kind of skiing from fast to steep, from glades to bowls. Like all Okanagan resorts, it enjoys an embarrassment of snowy riches, with an annual average of more than 225 in (565 cm).

Two high-speed quad chairs disperse traffic fairly evenly over the 500 acres (200 ha) of groomed trails and another 500 acres of bowls and glades, with supplemental triples and doubles well located to fill in the gaps away from the most heavily skied runs. One of these is the Alpine T, which runs to the summit ridge, and after a tricky little traverse gives access to the super-steep Cliff, a legendary freefall wall that regularly lures the daring.

Elsewhere, the triple chair tends to run uncrowded up to the heavily treed powder traps of the south ridge, but mostly, Big White serves up heaps of beautiful wide-open cruising that all eventually winds up down at the village center.

Not that a little exploring won't pay dividends, especially if you check out the backside bowls of the East and West Peaks. Try the trees as well, especially down Powder Gulch and Surprise. Ski the full measure of Big White—it's a wide-shouldered beast that begs discovery, and by limiting yourself to the 51 marked trails, you can miss out on some of the tastier treats that the mountain offers.

The Ridge Rocket Quad gives you access to the most varied skiing, including giant slalom cruisers like Roller Coaster, Speculation and Villager, or steep, bumpy pitches like Dragon's Tongue and Goat's Kick. There's also the Paradise Glades to play around in; the snow is deep and soft in this area, and the scattered trees add an extra thrill.

The Bullet Quad runs directly up from the

Whitefoot Lodge and gives you access to the mostly intermediate terrain on the north shoulder of the mountain. From there you can take the Alpine T up to the runs of the Cliff. After warming up on the cruising runs off the Ridge or Bullet quads, you might want to head for the expert terrain off the Powder Chair and the new Whitefoot Chair. It's mostly above-treeline bowl skiing, and I think it's some of the best skiing at Big White. Powder Bowl and Whitefoot Trail drop from the ridge in great rolling waves, broken only occasionally by clumps of stunted, snow-shrouded trees. The trails pitch and roll, then plunge into the trees to the bottom of the Whitefoot Chair.

Some days the new snow is so deep that the vertical off the Powder Chair is not sufficient to get you cooking. That's when it's time to head for the Cliff. As one local remarked, "When it's good, it's just like helicopter skiing." This wall of steepness is reached via the Bullet Chair and then the T-bar, where you take a long traverse until you stand on the edge of 1,000 vertical ft (305 m) of very steep, very deep powder. Before you plunge down you'll see the Monashees sparkling in the distance, and far below the dark forested lower half of the mountain. It's the place where all the virtues of Big White's skiing become apparent, and it's a view that sticks in your mind like few others.

Parachute Bowl was recently opened up on the north side of the mountain adjacent to the Clif, and it's without doubt the most radical skiing on the mountain. It's unrelentingly steep—the lower half was the site of the 1991 Canadian Speed Skiing Championships—and you reach it through some narrow rock bluffs before launching into more than 50 acres (20 ha) of bowl skiing. It's extreme skiing, so don't venture over there unless you are hard-core.

HOW TO SKI BIG WHITE

Novices

Start with a couple of warm-up runs off the Plaza Quad, then take the Ridge Rocket and ski Serwa's Salute. Head back up the Ridge, take Easy Out, and ski over to the Bullet Express, then take a combination of Sun Run and Sundance.

Intermediates

Take the Bullet Express and pick either Mervyns, Easter Gulley or International for some nice wide-open cruising terrain. For some open-terrain bowl skiing, head for the Alpine T-bar and try either Sun Run or Enchanted Forest. If the snow is too deep, you can bail out on the Ridge Run and pick your way down to Villager Track or Easy Out, which are protected by trees. From the Ridge Rocket turn left and head down Mogul Track, then cut under the chair to Perfection all the way down to the base.

Experts

From the Ridge Rocket turn left and head down the steep and narrow Dragon's Tongue or Goat's Kick. Next take Shakey Knees down to the Powder Chair, then try Flagpole or Corkscrew. Head back over to the top of the Ridge Rocket via Trapper's Trail, ski down to the bottom of the Alpine T-bar, then head for the really steep stuff on the Cliff, Pegasus or Parachute Bowl.

WHERE TO STAY

Staying on the mountain makes the most sense, not just to eliminate the 62-mi (100-km) round trip to Kelowna but because the hotels and condos of Big White Village are both convenient and moderately priced. Most, however, are not luxurious, and some are starting to show their age. You have your choice from a simple hotel room right up to one-, two- or three-bedroom suites, all comfortable enough to rest your weary head, and all within walking distance of the village center and its amenities.

All reservations for the following hotels can be made through the resort's central reservation number at (604) 765-8888. Payment can be made by Visa, MC or Amex.

Moderate

Das Hofbrauhaus
One of my favorites on the mountain, Das Hobrauhaus has a nice feeling about it. The units are bright, well appointed, and they face either the mountain or out over the enclosed courtyard (and the only swimming pool on the mountain). Rooms come in one and two bedroom sizes, some with kitchens, and there's a hot tub and sauna on the premises. Rates $60–$75 per person.

Moguls
The newest and the nicest condo units on the mountain, ranging from studio to three-bedrooms. All suites have a kitchen, fireplace and satellite TV. Some

also have en-suite sauna. The furnishings are a cut above the average. Good for one or two couples. Rates $40–$65 per person.

Ponderosa Motel
Perhaps the best bet for families, the Ponderosa has one- to three-bedroom units, full kitchens, comfortable furnishings, TVs and laundry facilities. Also has hot tub and sauna facilities. Rates $55–$65 per person.

Ptarmigan Inn
Right behind the Whitefoot Inn, the Ptarmigan has a mix of one- to three-bedroom units, all with kitchens. There's nothing fancy here, just basic family accommodation. A hot tub and sauna are available. Rates $30–$40 per person.

Tamarack Inn
The Tamarack's location in the middle of the village makes it both convenient and noisy. But if you don't mind late-night partyers passing by your window, its units are better than most on the mountain: roomy and fairly well furnished, with one or two bedrooms, some with fireplace and balcony. There are also a few rooms with saunas. Rates $55–$65 per person.

The Whitefoot Lodge
This is front and center on the mountain, and while it's not fancy it is well equipped and the hub of all activity. Has hotel rooms and condo units up to three bedrooms, with kitchen or kitchenette, and some have a fireplace. Be warned, this is a busy and noisy spot. If getting to bed early is important, stay elsewhere. Rates $40–$50 per person.

In Kelowna
Moderate
Capri Hotel
A huge, sprawling neo-gothic structure, the Capri is a 183-room full-service hotel that's an institution in Kelowna. The rooms are large, usually with two double beds, and facilities include sauna, hot tub, lounge and dining room. Also has some suites with kitchens. Rates $78–$225 per person.
1171 Harvey Ave. Tel (604) 860-6060
Visa, MC, Amex, Diners, enRoute

Hotel Eldorado
If you're looking for a stylish place to stay, this rebuilt heritage inn is all that and more. It's small, with just 20 rooms, and everything is done with taste and attention to detail. It doesn't have many amenities, but it is situated right on Lake Okanagan. Rates $89–$109 per person.
500 Cook Rd. Tel (604) 763-7500
Visa, MC, Amex, enRoute

Okanagan Seasons Resort
Although primarily a summer resort on the shore of Lake Okanagan, this is the swankiest spot in town. It's also one of the largest, with 70 rooms and suites. Some have kitchens, and there's a dining room. Also has a pool, sauna, jacuzzi and other luxuries. If you want to be catered to, this is your best choice in town. Rates $55–$75 per person.
1580 West Hwy 33. Tel (604) 860-5707
Visa, MC, Amex, Diners, enRoute

WHERE TO EAT
If you're staying on the mountain, it makes little sense to drive into Kelowna for dinner, but given the limited dining choices on-site, you may feel compelled to go at least once. Kelowna does have a wide range of good dining spots.

A note: There is a grocery store and liquor store on the mountain, but if you plan to do a lot of cooking (or drinking) in your room, better to pick up your goods in Kelowna. The selection is far better—especially for fresh vegetables and fruit— and the prices are definitely cheaper.

Moderate
Barclay's Restaurant
Casual dining with mostly standard stuff, including burgers, steak, chicken and pizza. Also does some daily specials, and is a good spot for hearty appetites and family groups.
In Das Hofbrauhaus. Tel 765-5611
Visa, MC, Amex

Snow Shoe Sams (Fireside)
The only fine dining spot on the mountain, and it has great atmosphere to boot, with a crackling fireplace and candle-lit tables. The menu is part continental and part North American, with items like Cornish game hen, pasta dishes and steaks. Suited to couples or quiet groups, and the only place where you can really get away from the packaged vacation crowds.
Next door to the Whitefoot Lodge. Tel 765-1416
Visa, MC, Amex

The T-Bar Bistro
A good spot for lunch on the mountain, or for grabbing some sandwiches to take back to your condo. Has a good variety of special coffees and other treats, and it's a little quieter than the other lunch spots on site.
In the Whitefoot Lodge. Tel 765-3101
Visa, MC, Amex

Whitefoot Restaurant
Family-style dining with all the standard fare, including roast beef, chicken, pizza and daily specials. Nothing too fancy, but ideal if you have a brood of hungry youngsters to feed.
In the Whitefoot Lodge. Tel 765-2414
Visa, MC, Amex

In Kelowna
Expensive
The Guisachen House
This is definitely the upscale dining spot in Kelowna, a tad on the expensive side, but elegant. Located in an 1890s house, it has a varied continental menu, with all white linen, crystal and open fireplaces. The desserts are worth the price of admission.
1060 Cameron Ave. Tel 862-9368
Visa, MC

Le Papillon
A stylish Kelowna restaurant catering to a rapidly growing yuppie retirement crowd. It's small, the service is first-rate, and the menu mainly a mix of seafood and pasta with some other specials. A good wine list of Okanagan

vintages and a pleasant atmosphere.

375 Leon Ave. Tel 763-3833

Visa, MC, Amex

Moderate

The Keg

Yet another of the ubiquitous chain, but locals swear that this one in downtown Kelowna is one of the better ones. Good standard fare with an emphasis on red meat and chicken.

274 Lawrence Ave. Tel 763-5435

Visa, MC, Amex, Diners, enRoute

P.J.'s All Star Café

The decor and the music make this a fun spot. It has a varied menu of items from fajitas to stir-frys, along with designer burgers, good wings and interesting daily specials.

In Orchard Park (the largest shopping mall in the B.C. Interior, with 300 stores), 2271 Harvey. Tel 861-5354

Visa, MC, Amex

Talos

One of my favorite spots in Kelowna. It's a smallish and well run family-owned restaurant specializing in hearty helpings of Greek food. The salad, as you might expect, is excellent. Don't miss the baklava.

1570 Water St. Tel 763-1656

No cards

NIGHTLIFE

On the mountain the nightlife scene is fairly limited, but downtown Kelowna fairly hops at night.

Loud and Lively

Loose Moose

Upstairs in the Alpine Centre, this is the best place for after-ski unwinding. It's always crowded, usually has live entertainment, and sometimes has impromptu dancing.

Rosa's on the Ridge

This is part bar, part lounge and part nightclub, with a similar mix of entertainment. Somewhat reminiscent of Berlin in the thirties. Karaoke is big—watch for Rosa to lead the way—and stand-up comics are regular entertainers, along with musical duos. A real mixed bag, and lots of fun.
In Das Hofbrauhaus. Tel 765-8888

Mellow

Upstairs in Snow Shoe Sams

A good spot to settle down in front of the fire, look out the windows at the snowy peaks, and sip a special coffee or liqueur. Light music in the background, lovers and other strangers in the foreground. Tel 765-1416

In Kelowna
Loud and Lively

Flashbacks

Live bands, flashing lights, mega-decibel sound and a busy dance floor make this place a prime attraction for the 25-and-up—not far up—set. Doesn't really get rocking until later, so if you plan to return to the mountain, bring a designated driver.
1268 Ellis St. Tel 861-3039

O.K. Corral

Strictly cowboy time at the O.K., with live bands, a vast dance floor for whirling your partner about, and lots of stetsons, checkered shirts and cowboy boots. A fun spot for some down-home music and entertainment.
1978 Kirschner Rd. Tel 763-5554

Splashes

Discos come and go in Kelowna, and one of the

**BIG WHITE/KELOWNA—
USEFUL TELEPHONE
NUMBERS**
(area code 604)

Kelowna Hospital 862-4000

Visitor and Convention
Bureau 861-1515

Kelowna Cabs 762-4444 or
762-2222

Kelowna Bus and
Transportation 860-8121

Hertz Rent-a-Car 860-7808

latest is Splashes, with a mix of rock and roll and Top 40 favorites. The crowd tends to be thirtyish, single and primed for action.
275 Leon Ave. Tel 762-2956

Mellow

McCullough's Station

One of my favorite places in Kelowna, if not the entire Okanagan. Located in an apple orchard on the outskirts of town, it's hard to find but worth the effort. It's a brand-new replica of a 1900s railway station complete with vaulted ceilings and a 40-ft mahogany bar. It's always packed with locals and tourists, plus it has the usual bar games such as darts and shuffleboard. Outside it's fieldstone, wood and glass—inside it's decorated with old pictures of the area.
At the corner of KLO and McCullough roads. Tel 762-8882

DIVERSIONS

Parapenting

Parapenting is the fine art of jumping off a cliff with a kite strapped to your back. It's big in Europe and claiming its devotees over here. You don't have to try it alone, though. Wayne Betrand, head of the Big White ski patrol, operates Aerial Sensations Paragliding and is a certified instructor. He'll take you in tandem off the Cliff, if you've got the nerve and about $40. If you like bungy jumping, you'll love this. Call 765-2FLY.

Down on the Boardwalk

If you still have energy left in your legs after a day on the slopes—or you have youngsters with more activity on their minds—the Boardwalk roller skating center is a fun spot, with loud music, couples skating arm in arm, and an atmosphere that's pure Coney Island. Skate rentals are available. 940 McCurdy St. Call 765-3622.

THE KOOTENAYS

HOW TO GET THERE
By Plane: Rossland and
nearby Trail are about 385 mi
(620 km) from Vancouver
and Calgary. Vancouver and
Calgary airports are served
by major airlines, with
connections from most
major centers. Spokane
Airport, in Washington, is
about 125 mi (200 km)
south. From Vancouver,
Calgary or Edmonton, Air
B.C. and Time Air fly into
Castlegar Airport, and from
there it's about a 30-minute
drive to Rossland.

By Car: From Vancouver take
Hwy 3 east through Hope
and Osoyoos to Grand Forks.
Take Hwy 3B into Rossland.
From Calgary take Hwy 2
south to Hwy 3 west through
Cranbrook and Creston into
Rossland.

By Bus: Greyhound Bus Lines
runs regular daily service
from Calgary and Vancouver
into Trail.

The Kootenay region of British Columbia is tucked into the south-central portion of the province, east of the Okanagan Valley and running north from the U.S. border to Revelstoke. Three mountain ranges tower over the 95-mi-long (150-km) Kootenay Lake, the Monashee Mountains to the west, the Purcells to the east, and the Selkirks driving a wedge up the middle.

Skiing began in this area about a century ago, when Norwegian gold mine workers began seeking winter recreation on the snowy mountains that surrounded them. A strapping miner by the name of Olaf Jeldness set the pace, organizing and winning the first Canadian championships with a time of slightly more than eight minutes for a two-mile-long downhill course that finished in the town of Rossland. Today, high above the quiet gentle streets of that mining community, is Red Mountain, an unpretentious resort that to my mind is truly one of the great undiscovered pure skiing experiences in Canada.

RED MOUNTAIN

Box 939
Rossland, B.C.
V0G 1Y0
Tel (604) 362-7384

RED MOUNTAIN— STATISTICALLY SPEAKING

Base Elevation:
3,888 ft (1185 m)

Summit Elevation:
6,688 ft (2038 m)

Vertical Drop:
2,800 ft (855 m)

Skiable Terrain:
2,500 acres (1000 ha)

Number of Trails: 30

Longest Run: 4.5 mi (7.2 km)

Lifts & Capacity: 1 triple,
2 doubles, 1 T-bar;
2,500 skiers per hour

Daily Lift Ticket: $32
Weekly: $139 (5 days)

Annual Snowfall:
300 in (750 cm)

No. Days Skiing 91–92: 116

Snowmaking: None

Terrain Mix:
N 20%, I 35%, E 45%

Snow Phone: 362-5500

About every 20 years or so, a red-hot racer from Red Mountain snags the Olympic spotlight with a gold-medal performance that vaults Rossland and the ski resort into the limelight. Nancy Greene did it in 1968, then Kerin Lee-Gartner repeated the feat in 1992.

In between, Red Mountain keeps operating in its own unassuming way, occasionally playing host to World Cup races and occasionally launching another promising young Red Mountain racer onto Canada's national alpine ski team. It also garners rave reviews from those in the know for its impressive vertical, its prodigious snowfalls, its expansive terrain and its temperate climate.

It remains one of the least-known major-league ski areas in the entire country. It is also, in my opinion, one of the very best. Sure, it's somewhat isolated and not the easiest place to get to. It does have a reputation for being an experts-only ski area. And maybe it doesn't have the extensive base area development that even lesser-known resorts such as Fernie or Kimberley have. But what it does have is some of the finest, pure fall-line vertical that you'll ever ski. Plus a quality and quantity of snow—300-plus in (750 cm) annually—that matches anything in western Canada, and maybe even the entire continent.

Nearby Rossland is another gem in the wilderness. A wholesome, outdoorsy town of some 4,000, it lacks the nightlife glitz that some demand as part of the skiing experience, but it makes up for it in other ways. Prices are modest, the townsfolk are friendly, and the comfortable pace is just what you need after a day of burning your thighs out at Red Mountain.

THE SKIING

The resort of Red Mountain comprises two peaks, the round-shouldered Red Mountain, with its wide-open slopes and mostly intermediate terrain, and the more rugged full-tilt boogie, Granite Mountain. Red is the smaller of the two at just a shade over 5,000 ft (1525 m) and a vertical of 1,420 ft (433 m), while Granite rises 6,688 ft (2038 m) and yields a vertical of 2,800 ft (855 m). Together they provide a total of 30 marked trails—and at least that many again are unmarked—for a staggering 2,500 acres (1000 ha) of uncrowded and varied skiing.

That tremendous variety is maybe the key to this Kootenay resort. As one local observed, "It never ceases to amaze me with its endless options. You ski through this meadow, make a few turns, then you hit another meadow, and you think, 'Wow, I just went through that!' But then you make another few turns, then another meadow. Each time you think you've seen it all, and each time you get another surprise." Granite Mountain, for instance, is a 360-degree marvel of discovery, with everything from low-altitude tree skiing in dense spruce forest to exceptional open bowls, steep, narrow chutes, meadows filled with bottomless snow, and off-piste terrain that is among the most challenging on the continent. Many visitors liken the demanding runs of Granite to such legendary expert resorts of Wyoming's Jackson Hole, and indeed there are few resorts anywhere that can match Red Mountain's share of expert slopes, which by even the most modest count amounts to almost 50 percent of the skiable terrain.

Not that the intermediate or the more cautious expert can't enjoy the soft, spongy snow that blankets the twin peaks. Granite's Paradise area on the backside has some beautiful wide-open cruising through alpine meadows and a score of long, winding giant slalom runs. Likewise the front side of Red Mountain is primarily intermediate skiing, with wide boulevard skiing, spiced up with some short, dizzying chutes through the trees. And it's all so marvelously simple. Just three chairlifts and a T-bar take you to anywhere on both peaks; lineups don't exist at Red.

It's not a resort for everyone, though. Families might find it just a little too radical. If you're looking for luxury condo living with all the amenities, look elsewhere. And if you prefer easy sliding groomed runs with few surprises, they're not here. But for those who can settle into homespun creature comforts that positively reek of rustic, and then the following morning let their skis run through the deep snow and a healthy dose of vertical, Red Mountain is the place.

HOW TO SKI RED MOUNTAIN

Novices

Take the T-bar and follow either the T-bar Slope or Little Red Run. From the Granite Chair ski to Boardwalk to Silver Sheep to Long Squaw for a 5-mi-long (8-km) gently winding run through the trees and back to the base lodge.

Intermediates

Take the Red Mountain Chair to summit, veer right, pick up Upper Back Trail to Lower Back Trail, and then follow T-bar Slope to the bottom.

From top of Granite Chair take Main Run down to Jake's Slope—make sure you keep left and away from Granite Towers—then pick up Indian Flats for a fast run to the bottom. From the top of the Granite Chair head over to the Paradise area to Gambler—it's black diamond, but there's lots of room—then pick up Southern Belle.

Also try the powder fields, the mini-bowls and orchards for real variety.

Experts

Take the Red Chair to the back trails, then pick War Eagle (steep and bumpy), Sally's Alley or Dale's Trail. From the Granite Chair take either Southern Belle or Southern Comfort for high-speed vertical, then head for the meadows for deep snow and a taste of the trees. Gambler and Ruby Tuesday give you straight shots down the face.

On powder days try the slides, Powder Fields and Short Squaw, and when you're ready for a real surprise head for Beer Belly.

WHERE TO STAY

Rossland, a little over a mile (2 km) from Red Mountain, and Trail, about 6 mi (10 km) away, have a number of motels and hotels, though some of the best places to stay are closer to the mountain. There's no sign of a condo village at Red yet, although the owners do have plans for a small number of units. Meantime, some of my favorite accommodation in all of the Interior can be found right at the bottom of the mountain.

All accommodation in Rossland and the surrounding area can be booked through Red Mountain Central Reservations at (604) 362-7700; toll-free (U.S. & Canada) 1-800-663-0105. You can pay with Visa, MC or Amex.

Moderate

Ram's Head Inn

One of the most delightful small lodges I've stayed at anywhere. Built with honey-colored handhewn timbers, the Ram's Head is run by its builders and owners, Doreen and Dave Butler. There are just eight rooms, each with a private bathroom and a double bed piled high with down comforters. The place fairly crackles with ambience. A fire is always burning in the 8-ft-high granite fireplace, the smell of home cooking hangs in the air, and Doreen and Dave are everywhere taking care of your needs. Meals are served in the dining room, and you can relax in the sauna or hot tub or just lounge in front of the fire. Perfect for couples. Rates $63–$71 per person per night including lift tickets.

At the foot of Red Mountain, next to Red Shutter Inn. Tel (604) 362-9577

Visa, MC, Amex, Diners

Red Shutter Inn

The Red Shutter is a fine small lodge. Just as comfortable as its neighbor, it has six rooms with two double beds in each. Also has a communal living room, kitchen and barbecue. Great home-style cooking, a hot tub and usually a slightly younger crowd staying there. Rate $45 per person, including breakfast; kids under 10 stay free in same room as parents. Ski packages are available.

At the foot of Red Mountain, next to Ram's Head Inn. Tel (604) 362-5131

CK, T/CK, no cards

Uplander Hotel

A larger, more traditional hotel about a five-minute drive from the lifts. It's modern and bright, with 67 mountain-view rooms, some of them suites with kitchenettes. Also has a dining room, pub, underground parking and hot tub. It's big, friendly and convenient, right in the heart of Rossland. Rates $68–$72 per room.

1919 Columbia Ave. Tel (604) 362-7375

Visa, MC, Amex, Diners

Inexpensive

Red Mountain Motel

A standard motel, with 11 rooms and 10 classic A-frame cabins out back. If you like rustic, go for one of those. They include cooking facilities and can handle up to eight people. The motel rooms are fairly large, with two double beds. Has a restaurant, lounge and sauna. Rate $60 per room.

At the foot of Red Mountain. Tel (604) 362-9000

Visa, MC

Scotsman Hotel

Aye, there's nothing quite as frugal as the Scotsman. A no-frills, no-pretenses place with 44 basic motel units, some of them suites with kitchenettes. About 2 mi (3 km) from the mountain and half a mile (1 km) from Rossland. Has a nifty 20-person outdoor hot tub. Rates $50–$55 per room.

1199 Hwy 3B. Tel (604) 362-7364

Visa, MC, Amex, Diners, enRoute, Discover

Bed & Breakfast

Angela's Place

Two bedrooms and two suites. The ground-floor suite is big enough for six people, the upper suite ideal for a couple. Also has lounge, hot tub and kitchen with do-it-yourself breakfast fixings. Rate $40 per person.

1520 Spokane St. Tel (604) 362-7790

CK, no cards

Heritage Hill

A beautifully renovated turn-of-the-century home with polished wood floors, beamed ceilings and stained-glass windows. Just four bedrooms (and two bathrooms) plus a living room. Hearty English breakfast served. Rate $40 per person.

1345 Spokane St. Tel (604) 362-9697

CK, no cards

WHERE TO EAT

Moderate

Louis Blue Room

Done up with high walls around booths on different levels. The menu is fairly

traditional, with steaks, lobster and a smattering of French cuisine plus daily specials. The homemade desserts are exceptional, and so is the view of the mountain from the giant picture window.
In the Uplander Hotel, 1919 Columbia Ave. Tel 362-7375
Visa, MC, Amex, Diners

Rockingham's
An elegant spot in the heart of Rossland that I like because it's also casual. The menu is a mix of traditional favorites such as steak, seafood and pasta, but there's also a selection of some 30 appetizers, which can be made into a meal themselves. Great Caesar salad.
2061 Columbia Ave. Tel 362-7373
Visa, MC

Roundhouse Restaurant
Open for lunch and dinner, the Roundhouse has the most distinctive menu in town—especially for dinner. Vaguely continental, but with fresh local specialties such as the boneless breast of chicken stuffed with fresh blueberries, plus the more traditional steaks, pastas and seafood. Lunch includes homemade soups, special sandwiches and great burgers.
In the Flying Steam Shovel Inn, 2003 2nd Ave. Tel 362-5323
Visa, MC

Sunshine Café
The oldest restaurant in town is a popular spot with the locals. It seats about 30 people in two rooms. The menu is a mix of basic and exotic, ranging from pasta, burgers and steak to Mexican dishes, curry chicken and Malaysian egg rolls. Also has daily specials. A good place to grab some great muffins and an exquisite carrot cake for on-mountain snacks. Also try the huckleberry pie.
2116 Columbia Ave. Tel 362-7630
Visa, MC

Inexpensive
Gold Rush Book Store and Espresso Bar
Apart from its collection of new and used books, posters, prints and local art, the Gold Rush serves up the best specialty coffees in town. If you like cappuccino, espresso or special teas, you can sip while you browse. Also has

RED MOUNTAIN—
FIVE 5-STAR FAVORITES

Best Run for Vertical
First, Second, Third Slide

Best Overall Run
Main Run

Best Restaurant
Roundhouse Restaurant

Best Bar/Nightclub
Flying Steam Shovel Inn

Best Accommodation
Ram's Head Inn
Skats Petersen, Red Mountain

RED MOUNTAIN—USEFUL
TELEPHONE NUMBERS
(area code 604)

Chamber of Commerce
362-5222

Star Taxi 368-3336

Medical Clinic 362-7307

fantastic homemade baked goodies, and the occasional jam session by local musicians.
2063 Washington Ave. Tel 362-5333
Visa, MC

Kingsland Restaurant
The place for a good Chinese feed, and an excellent bargain if you have a family or budget-conscious group. The standard Chinese fare, plus some specialties like curried prawns and honey-garlic spareribs. For the more timid, there's burgers and red meat. Hearty portions and modest prices.
2032 Columbia Ave. Tel 362-7141
Visa, MC, Amex

NIGHTLIFE
Loud and Lively
The Flying Steam Shovel Inn
A great neighborhood pub housed in a heritage house built in 1867, during Rossland's last gold rush. It was restored in 1989 and is a great spot for hanging out, sipping suds, playing games and listening to music. Occasionally has live entertainment. Always has a good crowd.
2003 2nd Ave. Tel 362-5323

Powder Keg Pub
After skiing head for the Powder Keg, and if you like it stick around until the evening, when there's usually live entertainment. You won't find it cheek-to-jowl, but it is friendly and the place where you can meet locals. Also has pool tables and large-screen TVs.
In the Uplander Hotel, 1919 Columbia Ave. Tel 362-7375

Mellow

Louis Blue Lounge
A good laid-back place to sit, sip and relax. Mellow background music, big comfy chairs and a relaxing atmosphere.
In the Uplander Hotel, 1919 Columbia Ave. Tel 362-7375

DIVERSIONS

Parapenting
If the vertical at Red didn't get your adrenaline coursing, try a tandem parasail. A qualified instructor will take you aloft from the top of either Red or Granite—try Granite for the longer flight—and bring you safely down to ground zero. One flight costs between $30 and $45, but it's worth every cent. Call Sky High Parapenting at 362-7384.

Ainsworth Hot Springs/Nelson
The hot springs at Ainsworth were discovered by the Kootenai Indians several hundred years ago, but more recently visitors have been rediscovering their soothing mineral-rich waters. They are about a 2 1/2-hour drive from Rossland, on the west arm of Kootenay Lake, and if you feel like taking a day off from the slopes, it's well worth the visit. The hot springs are in a large horseshoe-shaped cave, and the water bubbles at a constant 104° to 110°F (40° to 43°C). There's also a hotel on the site, if you get so relaxed you don't feel like driving back. For more information on Ainsworth Hot Springs write: Box 1268, Ainsworth Hot Springs, B.C. V0G 1A0, or call (604) 229-4212.

Nelson, just a 40-minute drive away, is worth a visit by itself. Without a doubt it's the prettiest community in all of B.C., with more than 350 restored heritage homes, in a spectacular setting beneath the mountains on the shores of Kootenay Lake.

THE B.C. ROCKIES

HOW TO GET THERE
By Plane: The nearest international airport is Calgary, which is served by major airlines with connections from major centers. The closest local airport is Cranbrook, which has connecting flights from Calgary via Air B.C. and Time Air.

By Car: From Calgary take Trans-Canada 1 west past Banff, then Hwy 93 south into Invermere. You can also take Hwy 2 south from Calgary to Hwy 3 west to Fernie and Kimberley. Each trip is about a three-hour drive. From Vancouver it is an eight-hour drive. Go east on the Coquihalla Highway to Hwy 1 east to Golden, then south on Hwy 95.

Tucked into the southeastern corner of British Columbia between the snow-laden Purcell Mountains and the towering Rocky Mountains, this skiing region has two points in its favor—besides incredible skiing.

First, it doesn't get the crowds that descend on Whistler, Banff or even the Okanagan. Heck, it doesn't get crowds at all. No snaking lineups of day-glo skisuits and tangled skis here.

Second, this region is called the warm side of the Rockies for good reason. Those towering ridges protect the slopes from the icy winds that roar across the prairies, and a light, dry snow blankets the area.

Three ski areas of note sit on either side of the Elk River valley, which pushes north from the U.S. border and merges into the Columbia River valley. Fernie Snow Valley occupies a ridge of high terrain just on the other side of the Crowsnest Pass, while 60 mi (100 km) farther north Kimberley Ski Resort nestles in the lee of the Purcell Mountains. Sixty mi (100 km) beyond, high above the Windermere valley, sits Panorama Ski Resort, also in the Purcells.

Box 788
Fernie, B.C.
V0B 1M0
Tel (604) 423-4655

HOW TO GET THERE

By Plane: The closest international airport is Calgary, which has connecting flights to Cranbrook Airport via Air Canada and Air B.C. Vancouver and Edmonton international airports have connecting flights to Cranbrook via Air B.C. and Time Air.

By Car: Fernie is a one-hour drive (60 mi/100 km) from Cranbrook via Hwy 3 south. From Calgary it's about a three-hour drive (200 mi/320 km) south on Hwy 2, then west on Hwy 3. A slightly faster route from Calgary is Hwy 2 south to Hwy 7 west, to Hwy 22 south to Hwy 3 west. From Vancouver it's about an eight-hour drive (600 mi/970 km) southeast on the Coquihalla Highway, then east on Hwy 1.

By Bus: Greyhound Bus Lines runs two daily trips to Fernie from Calgary.

Fernie Snow Valley is about 3 mi (5 km) outside Fernie, a mining town nestled in the verdant lowlands of the Elk River valley. As you begin the climb out of town, the Lizard Range, a 15-mi-long (24-km) picket fence of peaks, comes into view, and in one small section of this snow trap lie the bowls and trails of the ski resort. Many bowls, in fact, starting with the Lizard Bowl in the center flanked by Cedar Bowl to the right and Currie Bowl to the left. The bowls are what make Fernie Snow Valley special, along with the fluffy, deep snow that fills them.

How deep, you ask? How about 250 in (600 cm) annually? That's 20 ft (6 m) of the lightest, softest, most skiable snow anywhere in the Interior, the kind of snow that falls all night and lies waiting for you in the morning, an unruffled duvet of fluffy, endless powder. And that annual average is just that—an average. Of the past three years, the winter of 1991–92 was the lightest, but the two years previous saw 370 in (928 cm) and 352 in (882 cm) fall respectively, including one incredible period in 1990–91 when the resort received snow on 97 days.

The bowls occupy the upper part of the Lizard Range, mostly above the treeline, while the lower half of the Polar Bear and Grizzly Peaks provide long and winding trails down through the heavily forested lower slopes to the base area. Three chairs, a quad, a triple and a double radiate out from the base, carrying you to the open alpine basins.

The base area at Fernie is as pretty and uncomplicated as the skiing layout, with an assortment of accommodation ranging from condominiums to hotels. Nearby Fernie is an equally neat, generic western Canadian, no-frills town of about 8,000. Many folks opine that Fernie Snow Valley is one of the best-kept skiing secrets in the

Base Elevation:
3,500 ft (1065 m)

Summit Elevation:
5,900 ft (1800 m)

Vertical Drop:
2,400 ft (730 m)

Skiable Terrain:
800 acres (320 ha)

Number of Trails: 40

Longest Run: 3 mi (5 km)

Lifts & Capacity: 1 quad,
1 triple, 1 double, 4 surface;
7,000 skiers per hour

Daily Lift Ticket: $30
Multi-day: $56 (2 days)

Annual Snowfall:
250 in (600 cm)

No. Days Skiing 91–92: 134

Snowmaking: None

Terrain Mix:
N 25%, I 40%, E 35%

Snow Phone: 423-4655

west. Still, it's becoming a popular destination for skiers seeking the kind of friendly, low-key western ski holiday that is in distinct contrast to the glitz and glamour of Whistler.

THE SKIING

At Fernie Snow Valley there are 40 marked trails, two bowls and extensive tree skiing, for a total of more than 800 acres (320 ha) of skiable terrain. At the south end of the ridge is Lizard Bowl, a wide-open snow field that is primarily intermediate terrain that falls for about 700 vertical ft (214 m) into the lower, more heavily treed runs of the mountain. There the runs are wide and straightforward, with just the right amount of steepness. You can ride the El Quad Chair for the glade runs, or head over to the Bear T-bar and traverse the top of the bowl until you find the route down that suits your mood.

To the north of the Quad Chair and above the Bear T-bar is Cedar Bowl, a steeper, snowier expert's paradise that features sharp, short chutes and some of the resort's double black diamond runs. Below the bowl are more of the Fernie tree runs; most noteworthy is Boomerang, a tight, narrow trail that snakes through the trees. Fernie regular Bob Jamieson describes Boomerang as "amongst 50 of my favorite turns in all of western skiingdom."

Two other bowl areas will someday be part of an expanded Fernie Snow Valley. To the south beyond the Lizard Bowl is Currie Bowl, and beyond that Timber Bowl, which skiers who have ventured there describe in almost reverential terms: perfect pitch, bottomless snow, big trees and outrageous skiing.

HOW TO SKI FERNIE

Novices

Take the Deer T-bar and from the top—about one-third of the way up the mountain—there's a choice of three wide-open, groomed trails. Meadow is wide and easy, Deer and Incline are a little steeper and narrower, but still easy sliding. You can also take the Quad Chair up to the higher elevations, where you pick up either Dipsy or Incline for long runs back to the base.

Intermediates

Take the El Quad Chair to the area just below the bowls. From there you can ski some nice cruising runs through the trees. Pick either Lizard or Holo Hike for long straight-away cruising, or pick some of the shorter, steeper pitches that cut through the trees. Next ski down from the Quad terminus to the Boomerang triple chair and go up to the Cedar Bowl area. From there take North Ridge. For a taste of that Fernie powder, ride the Bear T-bar, then the Face Lift, and take Cruiser.

Experts

You want to get high up in the Lizard or Cedar bowls via the El Quad Chair, the Bear T-bar and then the Face Lift. It's steep up there, and the snow is deepest. If you're looking for bumps, try Boomerang Ridge, from the Boomerang Chair. If it's vertical you want, head for the Face Lift, then take the Lizard Traverse across the bowl to Sky Dive or Decline. For the best powder take the Face Lift and then the Cedar Traverse across Cedar Bowl to either Cedar Centre or Snake Ridge.

WHERE TO STAY

Base-area accommodation at Fernie is all ski-in/ski-out, with three lodges offering some moderately priced variety.

All accommodation at the resort and in Fernie can be booked through Fernie Central Reservations at (604) 423-9284.

Moderate

Griz Inn

This is the centerpiece of the resort's base facilities, and my favorite place to stay. It's a handsomely designed wooden lodge with clocktower, balconies and

a sprawling deck. It has 36 condo units in one- to four-bedroom layouts, some with kitchens, and eight new hotel rooms, which, with a double bed plus bunks, suit families. Also has an indoor swimming pool, two outdoor hot tubs, sauna and laundry facilities. Rates $285–$400 for five-day package that includes lift tickets, ski instruction, three breakfasts and two dinners.
Ski Area Rd. Tel (604) 423-9221
Visa, MC, Amex

Timberline Condominiums
These condos are about half a mile (1 km) away from the base area, and although you have to take the shuttle bus up to the lifts, you can ski back down to the condos at the end of the day. There are 30 units, and they could be considered the most luxurious at the resort. There's a mix of one- and two-bedrooms, all with full kitchen, fireplace and balcony. Also has outdoor jacuzzis. Rates $100–$130 for one-bedroom unit.
Tel (604) 423-6878
Visa, MC

Wolf's Den Mountain Lodge
The newest lodge at the resort has 42 standard hotel rooms and not much else. It's a convenient place to stay, and does have indoor hot tubs, a games room, exercise area and laundry facilities. Rates $50–$70 per person including lift tickets.
Ski Area Rd. Tel (604) 423-9202
Visa, MC, Amex

Nearby Fernie has a variety of small, comfortable hotel and motel options.

Moderate
Cedar Lodge
A full-service hotel, with 48 rooms (some with kitchen) that can accommodate from two to six people. It has one of the better dining rooms in town. Also has indoor pool, jacuzzi and sauna. Rates $200–$240 per person for five-night package including lift tickets.
1101 7th Ave, off Hwy 3. Tel (604) 423-4622
Visa, MC, Amex, Diners

Park Place Lodge
The best hotel in town, the Park Place is about a five-minute drive from the slopes and has 40 good-sized hotel rooms, plus amenities that include a restaurant, pub, indoor swimming pool, jacuzzi, sauna and a beer and wine store. It's a good spot if you're looking for hotel-style service and convenience. Rates $220–$235 for a five-night package that includes lift tickets.
Tel (604) 423-6871
Visa, MC, Amex, Diners, enRoute, Discover

Inexpensive
Barbara Lynn's
A comfortable B&B with just eight rooms. Rate $25 per person; $115 for a group of six.
39 Mt. Klauer Rd. Tel (604) 423-6027
No cards

Hi 3 Lodge
A basic motel facility, with standard rooms, some of which have kitchenettes. Also has a jacuzzi and sauna. Rates $185–$200 for five-day package including lift tickets.
Hwy 3. Tel (604) 423-4492
Visa, MC, Amex, Diners, CB, Discover

The Log Inn
I like the country setting of this place, and it's only a 10-minute drive to the resort. There are 10 comfortable rooms with period furnishings. Also has a sauna. Rates $25–$30 per person per night.
25 Anderson Rd. Tel (604) 423-7524
Visa, MC

WHERE TO EAT
Expensive
The Old Elevator
No doubt about it, the Old Elevator is the best dining spot in town. Also the most expensive, but by big-city (or Whistler) standards, it's reasonable. Its wide-ranging menu runs from king crab to steaks, with lots of interesting specialties. The decor is cedar and stained glass, with two fireplaces providing

a warm glow and an ambience that's hard to beat.

291 1st Ave. Tel 423-7115

Visa, MC, Amex, Diners, enRoute

Moderate

The Cedar Dining Room

Some locals suggest this is the best eatery in town at the best prices, and I can't disagree. The prime rib is especially good, and the salad bar is worth a visit alone.

In the Cedar Lodge, 1101 7th Ave, off Hwy 3. Tel 423-4622

Visa, MC

The Griz Inn Dining Room

The main dining room at the inn has a varied menu of fish, fowl and beef vaguely described as continental. It's ultra-convenient if you're staying at the mountain. Good family dining.

Ski Area Rd. Tel 423-9221

Visa, MC, Amex

Inexpensive

Sky and Sea Café

For a place so far from the nearest ocean, the local claim that it serves the "best fish and chips in the world" seems a little outlandish. However, I tried it, and heartily concur. Also serves a mean stir-fry and some other house specialties. Great chow, great prices. Don't miss it.

1241 7th Ave. Tel 423-3131

Visa, MC

NIGHTLIFE

When I first arrived in Fernie and asked where the action was, one local wag suggested, "In Calgary—three hours away." Well, there are a few spots to let loose.

Loud and Lively

Buckaroos

For après-ski, Buckaroos is your best bet. It's a big round bar with floor-to-ceiling windows overlooking the slopes, and walls decorated with old skis and paintings by B.C. artist Jack Lee McLean. The music is usually taped, but occasionally on weekends there's live entertainment. Later on in the evening

**FERNIE—USEFUL
TELEPHONE NUMBERS**
(area code 604)

Chamber of Commerce
423-6868

Kootenay Taxi 423-4408

Fernie Taxi 423-4408

Sparling East Medical Centre
423-4442

the place hums, and theme nights produce some interesting entertainment value. While you're there, try the Griz Coffee.
In the Griz Inn, Ski Area Rd. Tel 423-9221

Park Place Pub
A popular après-ski spot, the pub is also busy later on in the evening, when it occasionally has live entertainment. Mostly, though, it's just a good, comfortable neighborhood pub with taped music, pool tables and electronic games.
In the Park Place Lodge. Tel 423-6871

The Valley Motor Inn
I don't recommend the Valley Inn for accommodation, but the bar does merit a note because it's one of the few places in town where you can dance up a storm. On busy weekends it brings in live bands; the rest of the time it's taped dance music and large crowds.
On Hwy 3. Tel 423-4411

DIVERSIONS

Taking a Gamble
Eureka, Montana, is about a 40-minute drive from Fernie, directly across the U.S. border, and its appeal lies mainly in its modest collection of gambling establishments and lively pubs and bars. You play a little poker, dabble in blackjack, arm wrestle with a slot machine or just enjoy the frontier town atmosphere with cheap drinks and food and a little duty-free shopping. This is not Las Vegas, but it is a fun spot for the evening. If you don't have a car, a taxi will take you there for about $15 a person.

Radium Hot Springs (see Panorama)

KIMBERLEY SKI AND SUMMER RESORT

Box 40
Kimberley, B.C.
V1A 2Y5
Tel (604) 427-4881

HOW TO GET THERE

By Plane: Kimberley is about a 20-minute drive from Cranbrook Airport. Air Canada has connecting flights from Calgary, and Air B.C. and Time Air have connections from Vancouver.

By Car: Kimberley is a three-hour leisurely, scenic drive through the Rockies via Hwy 2 south from Calgary to the historic Crowsnest Pass, then west on Hwy 3 to Hwy 93 north.

By Bus: Greyhound Bus Lines runs a daily service to Kimberley from both Calgary and Vancouver.

The Kimberley Ski Resort is about a mile (1.5 km) outside and 600 ft (180 m) above the small city of Kimberley, about 60 mi (100 km) north of the U.S. border and tucked into the lee of the Purcell Mountains, mother range of the legendary Bugaboos. It's a delightful western community that is a curious mix of its mining heritage and a more recently created Bavarian overlay.

The Bavarian blitz began over a decade ago, when the city decided that tourism, not mining, was the way of the future. The result is a curious cowboy/polka mélange of lederhosen and plaid shirts, pickup trucks and Tyrolean chalets, and the rattle of chainsaws competing with the accordion music piped into the street. Amidst it all, locals in cowboy hats and tourists in skisuits stroll beneath Happy Hans, a 10-ft-high Bavarian effigy that regularly emerges from a large cuckoo clock in the middle of the Platzl, the town's pedestrian mall. It sounds corny, but it all works.

And so does the resort, in a low-key way. There's nothing fancy about the Kimberley Ski and Summer Resort, just good big-mountain skiing on the eastern corner of North Star Mountain, rising from the Rocky Mountain trench. The ski area is laid out east to west across a broad shoulder of the mountain, and a large bowl area drops behind the 6,500-ft (1980 m) summit to the north.

Besides its varied terrain and steady if unspectacular annual snowfall, Kimberley is the kind of resort where you feel comfortable even if you're not sporting the newest boards or the flashiest ski duds. It's unpretentious, ever-challenging and just about as down-home as you can get.

THE SKIING

Kimberley is not big by western standards, with only

Base Elevation:
4,200 ft (1280 m)

Summit Elevation:
6,500 ft (1980 m)

Vertical Drop:
2,300 ft (700 m)

Skiable Terrain:
450 acres (180 ha)

Number of Trails: 34

Longest Run: 4 mi (6.4 km)

Lifts & Capacity: 2 triples,
1 double, 4 surface lifts;
6,000 skiers per hour

Daily Lift Ticket: $32
Multi-day: $90 (3 days),
$145 (5 days)

Annual Snowfall:
110 in (274 cm)

No. Days Skiing 91–92: 122

Snowmaking: 10%

Terrain Mix:
N 15%, I 60%, E 25%

Snow Phone: 427-4881

about 450 acres (180 ha), but its network of trails that criss-cross the broad, high ridge are a good mix of the steep, the long and the unforgiving for a total of almost 22 mi (35 m) of spectacular sliding.

Immediately above the base village area the Rosa Triple Chair climbs 6,500 ft (1980 m) to the top of some fine intermediate cruising grounds. Adjacent to the chair is a bit of a relic in these days of bubble-enclosed quad chairs, but the Maverick T-bar—the longest on the continent at 6,000 ft (1830 m)—serves its purpose well by taking you to the top of some wide-open trails that are perfect for getting the kinks out of your style and for getting your high-speed kicks. Maverick T-bar also takes you directly to the Kootenay Haus, a log structure that serves up a palatable on-mountain lunch and has a sundeck on which to recline and take in the stunning view of the Rockies on the other side of the Columbia River valley.

On the western side of the ridge is the Easter Triple Chair, which serves some shorter but alarmingly steep runs, including the Easter Run, which freefalls for 3,600 ft (1100 m) through progressively steeper terrain and larger moguls. The trees are a little denser on this side of the mountain as well, and many skiers are tempted to use them as slalom poles, but as one local suggested, "You don't ski the trees at Kimberley unless you like to brush your teeth with a lodgepole pine." Point taken. If you want some excitement in your skiing, just head for the backside after a traverse from the top of the Easter Chair. There you'll find half a dozen of the most sublime powder runs, ungroomed, choked with snow, and with enough pitch to take your breath away. Elsewhere there's Buckhorn, with its 2,300 ft (700 m) of vertical drop, and the shorter but no less entertaining Runt, Rung, Midget and Twilight.

Mix and match is the key at Kimberley. A little vertical here, some main-street cruising there, and a dose of the unexpected almost everywhere.

HOW TO SKI KIMBERLEY

Novices

Take the Rosa Triple Chair to the top, then veer right and ski past the Kootenay Haus to North Star Main, a wide-open cruising run. On the lower part of the run it gets a little steeper, but you can take the easy way out back to the base lodge. Or ride the Eastern Triple to the summit, then take the long winding Ridge Run.

Intermediates

Take the Buckhorn double to the top and ski down immediately under the chair on Buckhorn. This run has great even pitch and lots of room to build speed. Take the Easter Chair to the top, get off to the right and pick up Dean. Midway down, Dean splits in two: to the right is rolling, high-speed terrain, to the left is a steep, bump-filled gulley. Also take the Ridge across to Flapper or Easter.

Experts

Take Easter Chair to the top and ski down Easter directly under the chair. The top section is wide-open high-speed cruising, then it spills over into a steep and bumpy section.

Or head right from the top of Easter Chair and take the short but steep Maverick. If your knees are still in good shape, next head to the backside from Easter and try Jackpot, Twist, Vortex and Ruff. All are ungroomed and ultra-steep.

WHERE TO STAY

There's on-slope accommodation at the resort, plus a number of alternatives downtown.

Moderate

Inn West and Kirkwood Inn

These are one- and two-bedroom condo units, with loft, kitchen, fireplace and balcony. They are spacious and well appointed, and each unit has a mountain view. Great hotel-type rooms are also available. The nearby recreation center

has saunas, hot tubs, a games room and laundry facilities. Rates $62–$178. The five-day package is $275–$335 and is an excellent deal.
880 North Star Dr. Tel (604) 427-7616
Visa, MC, Amex

Mountain's Edge Inn
There are 42 one-bedroom units at the Mountain's Edge, and though they might not be considered luxurious, they are comfortable, well furnished and loaded with all the amenities, including kitchen, balcony, fireplace and satellite TV. There are pull-out couches, so each unit can accommodate four. Rates $55–$95; three-day packages are much cheaper.
930 Dogwood. Tel (604) 427-5381
Visa, MC, Discover

Purcell Condo Hotel
The Purcell is a collection of 56 one- and two-bedroom units, most of them with fireplace and kitchen. Good slopeside location, and great three- and five-day package rates that start as low as $65 per person including lift tickets.
Gerry Sorensen Way. Tel (604) 427-5385
Visa, MC

Rocky Mountain Condo Hotel
A combination of condo suites and smaller hotel rooms, the Rocky Mountain is a good spot for couples and families. Some of the larger units accommodate up to six people, and most include a fireplace and balcony. There's also a racquetball court and health club. Rates $55–$182.
Gerry Sorensen Way. Tel (604) 427-5385
Visa, MC

Silver Birch Chalets
This collection of two- and three-bedroom townhouse dwellings is my favorite on the mountain. The units are large enough to handle up to 10 people but comfortable enough for a couple. Each unit also has a small basement apartment, which is great if you're traveling with kids who want some space of their own. Complete with kitchen, fireplace, balcony and a great view. Rates $55–$261.
Dewdney Way. Tel (604) 427-5385
Visa, MC

In Kimberley

The Inn of the Rockies

Just three minutes from the center of town, the Inn is the best hotel around, and for those who don't need a kitchen but like the idea of hotel service and convenience, it's a great spot. Rooms are large, most come with two double beds, and there's a shuttle up to the resort. Rates $55–$75.

300 Wallinger Ave. Tel (604) 427-2266

Visa, MC, Amex, Diners, enRoute, Discover

WHERE TO EAT

Expensive

Chef Bernard's Kitchen

The menu is a combination of Swiss and French specialties, including great fondues and veal dishes. Chef Bernard does it up right, and it's one of my favorites.

170 Spokane St, in the Platzl. Tel 427-4820

Visa, MC, Amex, Diners, enRoute, Discover

The Old Bauren (Barn) House

This restored 1640 Bavarian farmhouse is a must for both excellent food and a trip back in time. Shipped over from Germany, then meticulously rebuilt, it's filled with handmade furniture and knick-knacks from the seventeenth century. The food is rustic German fare, from schnitzel to sausages, and it has its own bakery. It's one of my favorites. Don't miss it.

At the corner of Gerry Sorensen Way and Norton Ave. Tel 427-5133

Visa, MC

Moderate

Kalamazoo Restaurant

The alternative cuisine choice in town, the Kalamazoo has a cedar and fern motif and a menu that ranges from lasagna to crepes. Has great ribs and various daily specials.

418 304th St, South Kimberley (Marysville). Tel 427-7765

Visa, MC

The Miner's Den

Your best choice if you're feeding a family or if you just want some good old North American favorites at good old-fashioned prices. Has lots of different daily specials, and the Saturday night prime rib dinner is excellent.

In the North Star Day Lodge at the resort. Tel 427-4881

Visa, MC, Amex, Discover

Inexpensive

Aikman's Restaurant

A good family dining spot that features daily specials plus old favorites such as chicken, hamburgers and inexpensive steaks.

175 Deer Park Ave. Tel 427-3626

Visa

Mary's Kitchen

I've never met Mary, but her staff serve up a great inexpensive meal that tends toward the basic, at very basic prices. Good for the family or those on a budget (or into no-fuss dining).

342 Archibald St. Tel 427-3412

Visa, MC

NIGHTLIFE

Loud and Lively

Immediately after skiing most of the crowd heads for the bar in the North Star Day Lodge. It's not fancy, but the mood is exuberant, the beer flows and the music is loud.

Kimbrook Inn

A somewhat seedy hotel that draws a crowd at night not to sleep but to dance. Has live entertainment on weekends, and the rest of the time it's recorded

dance music.
2665 Warren St. Tel 427-7848

The Last Run

The Last Run can be either deadly quiet or wild with activity. The activity usually occurs only on Friday and Saturday nights, when there's live entertainment—mostly of a western variety—along with a large and boisterous crowd.
At the North Star Dining Centre. Tel 427-4881

Sullivan's Pub

A good neighborhood pub with all the usual pub attractions, including a stand-up bar, miscellaneous games and a chatty local crowd.
314 Ross St. Tel 427-5516

Mellow

The Inn of the Rockies

The lounge in this hotel is your best bet for a few drinks in a quiet setting. It occasionally books a live solo entertainer, but mostly you get just some mellow background music.
300 Wallinger Ave. Tel 427-2266

PANORAMA

Box 7000
Invermere, B.C.
V0A 1T0
Tel (604) 342-6941

HOW TO GET THERE

By Plane: Cranbrook Airport is about 80 mi (130 km) from the resort. Air Canada and B.C. Air have connecting flights from Calgary.

By Car: The 3 1/2-hour drive from Calgary via Hwy 1 west and Hwy 93 south takes you through three of Canada's best-known national parks—Banff, Yoho and Kootenay. The cutoff for Hwy 93 is about halfway between Banff and Lake Louise and takes you over the Rockies through Vermilion Pass. Or you can take a slightly longer route by staying with Hwy 1 through Kicking Horse Pass into Golden, then heading south on Hwy 95.

By Bus: Visitors on package tours will be bused directly from Calgary Airport to the resort. Greyhound Bus Lines runs daily service to Invermere, where a shuttle bus takes you up to the resort. There is no charge for the shuttle bus.

The village of Invermere on Lake Windermere was once better known as a summer destination for urban escapees from the Calgary region. But the emergence of Panorama Ski Resort in the early 1980s opened up the region to winter vacationers, and in recent years it has become a first-rate self-contained ski village with superb wide-open cruising terrain set amidst the Purcell Mountains.

Located 12 mi (19 km) above the valley, the resort is considerably different from its neighbors to the south. To begin with, Panorama is truly self-contained, with little or no interaction with the community of Invermere. There are virtually no day skiers at Panorama; most visitors come from farther afield on week-long packages and bed down on the mountain in one of the three hotel/condo complexes. Second, despite its location in the snow-rich Purcells, Panorama does not get the hefty snowfalls that blanket Fernie and Kimberley, so it compensates with one of the most extensive snowmaking systems in B.C. Seventy percent of its terrain is covered with artificial snow, and the result is firm, well-groomed trails of the kind most eastern skiers are more familiar with. And finally, Panorama lacks the bowl and tree skiing that other western resorts provide. It is, in short, an eastern-style resort in a western setting.

That doesn't mean there isn't some fine skiing to be had. Panorama does, after all, possess the third-highest vertical in Canada, at 3,800 ft (1160 m), and for those who enjoy wide-open, high-speed giant slalom cruising, it's hard to beat. What it does lack is variety. It's an up-and-down mountain with not much mystery and not too many options for exploring.

The base village is a terraced collection of some 275 hotel and condo rooms, interspersed with

Base Elevation:
3,200 ft (975 m)

Summit Elevation:
7,000 ft (2135 m)

Vertical Drop:
3,800 ft (1160 m)

Skiable Terrain:
300 acres (120 ha)

Number of Trails: 32

Longest Run: 1.9 mi (3 km)

Lifts & Capacity: 1 quad,
1 triple, 2 doubles, 3 surface
lifts; 6,800 skiers per hour

Daily Lift Ticket: $32
Weekly: $149 (6 days)

Annual Snowfall:
130 in (330 cm)

No. Days Skiing 91–92: 135

Snowmaking: 70%

Terrain Mix:
N 20%, I 60%, E 20%

outdoor hot tubs, barbecues and other resort amenities. It's convenient, compact and, some might suggest, just a tad boring. But it does work, and it works best for families, especially those seeking a first-time western ski experience.

THE SKIING

There's not a lot of mystery to Panorama: it's a straight-shot mountain with the third-highest vertical drop in B.C. and some of the fastest giant slalom cruising in the region. The vertical of 3,800 ft (1160 m) is the main reason Panorama is a regular stop for men's and women's World Cup races, and the groomed, hard-packed trails are easy to run from top to bottom.

Most of the 32 trails are clearly visible from the base area. A quad chair takes you to mid-mountain, then a triple chair takes you to the summit. You could ski those two lifts all day and experience most of the trail network, which makes it easy to keep track of the kids or the rest of your gang.

HOW TO SKI PANORAMA
Novices

Take the Quadzilla Chair or Toby Chair to mid-mountain and ski Horseshoe, Newtimer, Showoff or Hogsflats. These are all gentle, winding trails with lots of room and firm, groomed snow.

Intermediates

Take the Quadzilla Chair to mid-mountain and take a few warm-up runs on Powder Trail and Old Timer. Then take the Sunbird Chair to the top and run such long cruisers as Heaven Can Wait, Little Dipper, Silky and Outrider. From the Horizon Chair, take Skyline and Roller Coaster.

Experts

You can ski anywhere on the mountain, but pick the longest routes down, especially Roller Coaster to Fritz's Run, a non-stop thigh-burner that locals call the Panorama fitness test. Also take Fritz's and Whiskey Jack from the Sunbird Chair, or a combination of Tacky, Liftline and Downhill from the Horizon Chair. Also head up the Champagne T-bar to the start of the World Cup runs and try Schober's Dream, for full-tilt vertical, or Top of the World and Picture Perfect.

WHERE TO STAY

Most visitors to Panorama stay at the resort in either the hotel or a condo. It's more convenient, especially if you don't have a car. The village is pretty well self-contained, with restaurants, bars and assorted recreation, but it can be a little stifling, and for those who prefer flexibility or would like to explore the surrounding valley, there are some options in nearby Invermere and Radium.

All accommodations at Panorama can be booked through Central Reservations at (604) 342-6941, toll-free (U.S. & Canada) 1-800-663-2929. Payment can be made with Visa, MC, Amex, Diners and enRoute.

Moderate

Horsethief Lodge

The bigger and nicer of the two condo complexes at the resort, the Horsethief has 195 units ranging from one to three bedrooms. These are full-service units, not too fancy but filled with all the accessories. All units have a full-size kitchen and a fireplace and some have lofts. There's also underground parking and outdoor hot tubs. Rates $76–$315 per unit for 2–8 people.

Pine Inn Hotel

The only hotel at the resort, it's a good spot if you're traveling solo or in a couple. The rooms are a good size with two double beds, close to the lifts, and most have balconies that overlook the mountain. There are also some larger one-bedroom suites. It's a good spot, all woody and western in motif, and with some nice extras such as a hot tub and exercise room. Rates $65–$75 per unit for 1–4 people. Weekly packages start at about $300.

Toby Creek Lodge

Smaller than Horsethief and a little farther from the lifts, the Toby Creek tends to be quieter than other accommodation. The units are one- to three-bedrooms, and there are a number of standard-size hotel-type rooms. All the suites have a kitchen, fireplace and balcony. Plus there's underground parking, a dining room, indoor and outdoor hot tubs and saunas. Rates $76–$315 per unit for 2–8 people.

Off the Mountain

Radium Lodge

About a 20-minute drive from Invermere (and the Panorama Road), the Radium Lodge is a self-contained health spa with two outdoor pools, natural hot springs, saunas, exercise and massage facilities and 66 rooms. Clean, friendly and tastefully furnished, Radium Lodge is well worth the extra drive. It's perfect for those interested in aqua activities. Rates $65–$95 per unit.

On Hwy 93. Tel (604) 347-9622

Visa, MC, Amex, Discover

WHERE TO EAT

Expensive

Chalet Edelweiss

A restaurant that's worth driving into Invermere to experience. It has basically a Swiss menu with some other national specialties. The fondues are excellent and varied, and the rösti and raclette are to die for. Also has good veal and beef dishes.

934 7th Ave. Tel 342-3525

Visa, MC, Amex, enRoute

Strand's Old House Restaurant

It's worth getting down into Invermere just to dine at Strand's. Located in an old house, Strand's would be an outstanding dining spot in even the biggest city. In Invermere, it's the best in town. A superb continental menu with various house specialties, great service and an elegant setting. Try the pepper steak or the rack of lamb—you won't be disappointed.

818 12th St. Tel 342-6344

Visa, MC, Amex, enRoute

Moderate

Black Forest
If you enjoy schnitzel and other Germanic specialties, you'll like the Black Forest. It has a good varied menu, with excellent soups and daily specials. Also has entertainment.
At the junction of Hwys 93 & 95. Tel 342-9417
Visa, MC, Amex, enRoute

Toby Creek Dining Room
The best dining on the mountain, the Toby Creek has a great atmosphere enhanced by the crackling fire in the stone fireplace. A continental menu, featuring beef, lamb, fowl and fish.
In the Toby Creek Lodge at the resort. Tel 342-6941
Visa, MC, Amex, Diners, enRoute

Inexpensive

Heli-Deli
A good spot for take-out, including sandwiches, salads and soups. Mostly a lunchtime spot, but good if you just want to grab something fast and light to take back to the condo.
At the Heli-Pad at the resort. Tel 342-3889
No cards

The Lakeside Inn
The dining room in this Invermere hotel has your typical dine-and-dash fare, including superb fish and chips, ribs and chicken and hearty sandwiches. It's not fancy but it's definitely cheap and a good spot for that quick no-fuss meal.
3 Marian St. Tel 342-6711
Visa, MC, Amex, Diners

Starbird Restaurant
The place to take the family on-mountain. It has a varied menu of traditional North American specialties, including chicken, burgers and beef dishes. Nothing fancy, just good basic square meals.
In the Pine Inn Hotel. Tel 342-6941
Visa, MC, Amex, Diners, enRoute

NIGHTLIFE

Loud and Lively

Bud's Social Club and Boogie Parlour

If it's Saturday night and you're not at Bud's, you must be a) over 25; b) a parent with youngsters in tow; or c) happy with your significant other. Everyone else heads for Bud's. It's loud music, rampant hormones, and general disco debauchery.

In an old garage across from the Supersave in Invermere. Tel 342-0211

The Glacier

The on-mountain night spot for dancing and mingling. It doesn't really get going until after dinner, but then it can definitely hum depending on the makeup of the crowd. A DJ spins the tunes, and you provide the dancing.

Adjacent to the Pine Inn Hotel at the resort. Tel 342-6941

The Lakeside Inn

If you can handle the drive up and down the Panorama Rd, and you are under 30, head for the Lakeside. It's the choice of locals, and apart from the general conviviality there are pool tables, darts, video games, big-screen TVs and a giant stand-up bar. Just make sure you have a way home before committing yourself.

3 Marian St. Tel 342-6711

T-Bar and Grill

The place to head for after skiing, it's casual, loud and features impromptu dancing along with action on the pool tables. Has pub-style finger food and good music, and you'll feel right at home shelling the complimentary peanuts and throwing the shells on the floor. Also cooks at night.

In the Pine Inn Hotel at the resort. Tel 342-6941

Mellow

Fireside Lounge

If you like big comfortable chairs, a roaring fire and some innocuous background music, the Fireside is for you. A good spot for couples to linger, and for parents to get away from the kids for a while.

In the Toby Creek Lodge at the resort. Tel 342-6941

Strathcona Pub

I wouldn't call the pub quiet, but it is more typical of the stand-around-and-talk places. There's music in the background, a comfortable neighborhood pub atmosphere, darts, finger food and a good feeling about the place.

In the Horsethief Lodge at the resort. Tel 342-6941

DIVERSIONS

Heli Happiness

If you've never tried it but have always talked about it, this may be your best opportunity without mortgaging the family estate. And a half-day or a full day of heli-skiing at Panorama makes more sense when you consider that the lift-service skiing can become a little repetitive once you've skied every run on the mountain at least twice. R.K. Helicopter Skiing is located right on site at Panorama, and for the price of a week's lodging you can ski four or five runs that you'll remember for a lifetime. Groups of 11 plus a guide depart from the heli-pad daily, and your heli-day includes three to four descents and picnic lunch high up in the southern end of the Purcell Mountains. A day costs $349, and you don't have to be an expert to take the plunge. R.K. Heli-Ski just wants you to be able to ski an expert run in control, but not necessarily with finesse. Contact R.K. Heli Skiing at Panorama, or book in advance by writing Box 695, Invermere, B.C. V0A 1K0. Call (604) 342-3889.

Hot Spring Frolic

The Radium Hot Springs health spa and resort is a great spot for an afternoon of water sports. About a 30-minute drive from the mountain, it has two giant outdoor pools, natural hot springs, and a massage center. It's fun, squeaky clean, and the last word in healthy self-indulgence. One visit costs $2.75, a day pass is $5.25. Call (604) 347-9485.

Shopping and Dining Shuttles
Even though Panorama caters to most of your needs in the village, there are still those who get a little itchy at their confinement, and the resort runs regular shopping and dining shuttles free of charge down into Invermere. Take advantage of them. The town is a scenic lakeside community, with some interesting shopping and some great dining.

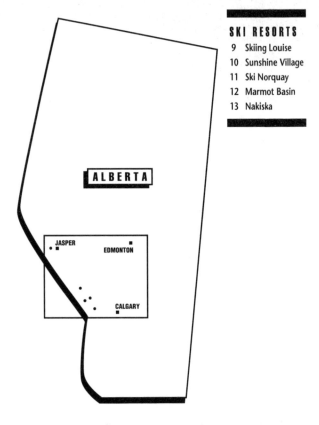

ALBERTA

JASPER   EDMONTON

CALGARY

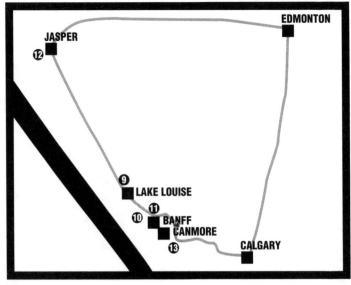

EDMONTON

JASPER
12

9
LAKE LOUISE
11
10 BANFF
CANMORE
13
CALGARY

ALBERTA

Around the world, the Rocky Mountains are arguably the best-known image of the Canadian wilderness. You can see them just ever so slightly the moment you step off the plane in Calgary, and as you begin the two-hour drive toward the gates of Banff National Park. In fact, there's no drive anywhere in Canada that builds the anticipation of heading for the mountains as much as the 75-mi (120-km) stretch from Calgary to Banff. Each turn of the four-lane highway brings the snow-capped range more clearly into view; each blacktopped mile passed heightens the sense of vastness that the towering glacier-riddled peaks produce. The Bow River courses by on your right, while to the left the soaring ridge of mountains looms larger as you leave the city far behind.

Stretching 320 mi (515 km), the Rocky Mountains form the spine of Alberta, a Continental Divide between Canada's two western-most provinces, providing a scenic feast that even the most gluttonous scenery hog will find hard to consume in a single helping.

It's that spectacular scenery that prompted wise men to set aside vast tracts of this special wilderness to form Banff National Park in 1885. It was the first such act of conservation, and Banff became the cornerstone of Canada's National Parks system. Today, the park is home to three of Alberta's best-known ski resorts—Sunshine Village, Lake Louise and Mount Norquay—and the two world-famous ski communities of Banff and Lake Louise.

To the west of Banff National Park are Kootenay and Yoho national parks, and to the north Jasper National Park, in the midst of which sits the baby brother of Banff, the tiny perfect mountain community of Jasper, and nearby Marmot Basin with its fine and uncrowded skiing. To the southwest is Kananaskis country, the site of three provincial parks and home to Nakiska at Mount Allan, the newest ski resort in Alberta, and the site of the skiing events at the 1988 Winter Olympics.

There are other ski areas in Alberta, but these five give the province its well-deserved reputation for fine skiing in the light, dry snow so typical of these 60-million-year-old mountains.

BANFF

HOW TO GET THERE
By Plane: Calgary International Airport is served by major airlines, with connections from major centers. Banff is 75 mi (120 km) north of Calgary; bus service runs from the airport or downtown Calgary.

By Car: Banff if an easy two-hour drive from Calgary; Lake Louise is another 30 minutes. From the airport follow signs for Trans-Canada 1. In Banff and Lake Louise, bus transportation is available between major hotels and the ski resorts, but for more flexibility and the option of sidetrips, you may want a car. Rent at the airport or in downtown Calgary; rental cars are in short supply—and pricier—in Banff.

By Bus: Three bus companies run regular shuttles to Banff from the Calgary area. From the airport, Brewster Transportation and Tours (403-260-0719) runs two daily shuttles and Pacific Western Transportation (403-243-4990) runs three daily shuttles; Greyhound Bus Lines (1-800-332-1016) runs three daily shuttles from downtown Calgary.

The postcard prettiness of Banff draws several million visitors year-round, yet curiously, considering its reputation for fine skiing, winter is considered the off-season. You might find that hard to believe when you stroll among the crowds along busy Banff Ave or try to make a reservation at one of the more popular restaurants, but the visitor count does nearly double in summer.

Just 10 mi (16 km) inside the gates of Banff National Park on the banks of the Bow River, this town of 6,500 is a sight to behold. Elk stroll the streets, a neat patchwork of tidy neighborhood streets have names right out of an Audubon guide, and peaks soar on all sides. Lofty Cascade Mountain, at nearly 10,000 ft (3050 m), is a granite sentinel at the northeast end of town; Mount Rundle climbs to 9,600 ft (2925 m) in the west; and Sulphur Mountain's heavily treed slopes rise 9,000 ft (2745 m) in the south. In their shadow Banff bustles, with all manner of hotels and other hostelries, restaurants, bistros, bars and shops giving the visitor a wealth of choice.

SKI NORQUAY

Box 1258
Banff, Alberta
T0L 0C0
Tel (403) 762-4421

HOW TO GET THERE
By Car: Mount Norquay is
5 mi (8 km), or a 10-minute
drive, from Banff. Take Bow
Ave at the east end of town,
cross the railway, and take
the switchback road up to
the base lodge area. Free
shuttle buses leave regularly
from the major hotels and
from the bus station.

THE SKIING

The first chairlift in western Canada was installed at
Mount Norquay back in 1948, and since then the
resort has been a fixture in Banff, albeit one that
until recently had a reputation of being a limited
expert-only ski area. This fearsome reputation was
based primarily on a daunting top to bottom mogul
run called Lone Pine, an unforgiving brute that was
legendary for its unrelenting vertical and monster
moguls. Daring locals and a few reckless visitors
relished the challenge, but for most skiers there was
little else to recommend this resort apart from its
proximity to town and some basic novice runs. If
visitors went to Norquay, it was more out of
curiosity.

That all changed in 1990 with the opening up of
the Mystic Ridge side of the mountain, a 70-acre (28
ha) addition of upper intermediate terrain that is
superbly laid out and serviced by two high-speed
quad chairs. All told, 12 new runs came as part of
the Mystic package, each one creatively curving
around the mountain for maximum pitch and length.
Now Norquay has more than enough variety to be a
reasonable alternative to Banff's two other resorts—
Sunshine and Lake Louise—and it's also the only
resort in the area to provide night skiing.

And yes, Lone Pine still beckons. For those who
relish a challenge, take a stab at becoming a member
of Club 35,000. To qualify for the gold pin award
requires 27 consecutive runs off the Norquay Chair
in one day—and that means one thigh-burning,
body-pounding run every 10 minutes.

Even if you don't take the challenge, you'll still
find that the new Norquay is a mountain worth your
attention.

SKI NORQUAY—STATISTICALLY SPEAKING

Base Elevation:
5,350 ft (1630 m)

Summit Elevation:
7,000 ft (2135 m)

Vertical Drop:
1,650 ft (502 m)

Skiable Terrain:
162 acres (65 ha)

Number of Trails: 25

Longest Run:
3,828 ft (1168 m)

Lifts & Capacity: 2 quads,
2 doubles, 1 surface lift;
6,300 skiers per hour

Daily Lift Ticket: $29.90

Annual Snowfall:
120 in (305 cm)

No. Days Skiing 91–92: 135

Snowmaking: 90%

Terrain Mix:
N 11%, I 45%, E 44%

Snow Phone: 762-4421

HOW TO SKI MOUNT NORQUAY

Novices

Stick to the Cascade Double Chair or the Sundance Tow; they service the easiest runs on the lower part of the mountain.

Intermediates

The Mystic Ridge is your playground. Stick to the mainly blue runs on your far left (as you look down the mountain). Trails like Imp and Bruno Gulley are fast and wide and long, with enough surprises to keep things interesting. The Spirit Quad also gives you some shorter intermediate runs.

Experts

No doubt about it, ski the old part of Norquay by riding the double chair. Get warmed up on North American and Memorial Bowl, then take your stab at Lone Pine. Experts will also enjoy the warp-speed cruising on the Mystic Ridge runs.

SUNSHINE VILLAGE

Box 1510
Banff, Alberta
T0L 0C0
Tel (403) 762-6500; in
summer 1-800-661-1363

HOW TO GET THERE

By Car: Sunshine is 10 mi (16 km) west of Banff on Trans-Canada 1. Drive 5 mi (8 km) along the Trans-Canada to the Sunshine Rd, then it's 5 mi (8 km) up to the Borgeau parking lot, where the Sunshine gondola takes you 3 mi (5 km) up to the main village at 7,000 ft (2135 m).

By Bus: Shuttle buses depart from the major Banff hotels four times each morning, with return trips from Sunshine at the end of the day. The cost for the shuttle bus is $1 each way but free if you have a Ski Banff/Lake Louise Pass.

There's probably not a better-known ski resort in all Canada than Sunshine Village. That it's one of the oldest has something to do with it, but the little resort that boasted a single rope tow back in the 1940s has come a long way.

Today it's a spectacular high-altitude alpine village straddling the Continental Divide, with high-speed lifts providing access to more than 780 acres (312 ha) of sublime skiing, most of which is above the treeline. Add to that an annual snowfall that can reach 30 ft (9 m), a ski season that can last from October to July, and 62 runs pouring down from three separate peaks, and you get some idea why the resort became the essential western Canadian ski experience for a whole generation.

For the majority of eastern Canadians, Sunshine Village was their first taste of big-mountain skiing. Robin Naismith, the guiding light behind Ski Can, a Toronto travel wholesaler, started some of the earliest modern-day ski charter packages to Sunshine more than 20 years ago, and although other destinations have developed a following in the ensuing years, Sunshine remains a top draw.

Sunshine, the only resort within the boundaries of Banff National Park that has on-slope accommodation, is accessible only via the gondola from the Borgeau parking lot 3,000 ft (915 m) below. The village is complete with restaurants, a shop or two, a bar, a cocktail lounge and assorted recreational amenities, including a 20-ft-wide outdoor hot tub. The 80-room Sunshine Inn is the centerpiece of the village. All of this is nestled in a pristine high-alpine setting, with the ski lifts and the skiing at your doorstep.

Considering its lofty isolation, the amount of Sunshine terrain that slots into the intermediate category is remarkably high. But even though it lacks

Base Elevation:
7,082 ft (2160 m)

Summit Elevation:
8,954 ft (2730 m)

Vertical Drop:
3,514 ft (1070 m)

Skiable Terrain:
780 acres (312 ha)

Number of Trails: 62

Longest Run: 5 mi (8 km)

Lifts & Capacity: 1 gondola,
1 quad, 1 triple, 4 doubles,
5 surface; 16,000 skiers per
hour

Daily Lift Ticket: $35

Annual Snowfall:
320 in (800 cm)

No. Days Skiing 91–92: 172

Snowmaking: None

Terrain Mix:
N 20%, I 60%, E 20%

Snow Phone: 762-6543

truly challenging terrain, most of us will find all we can handle in the long sweeping bowls that are its trademark. And in those bowls is some of the lightest, driest snow in western Canada—snow so abundant that skiing into July has become a tradition (albeit one that attracts more marketing hype than actual skiers).

THE SKIING

From the base village, the slopes of Sunshine fan out in a three-quarter circle of mostly above-treeline skiing on Lookout Mountain and Mount Standish. It's a lot of wide-open terrain that's filled with light, dry snow and has a superb view of the Rockies in all directions.

From the center of the village, the Angel Express, a high-speed quad, takes you above the treeline to the wide-open terrain that includes a mix of black diamond runs off to your left, some more forgiving intermediate runs down the middle of the snowpack, and a long, meandering beginner's trail to the far right. If you choose not to head back down to the village, a quick scoot down to the right will take you to the base of the Great Divide Chair, which carries you to the top of Lookout Mountain, at 8,954 ft (2730 m). The Great Divide actually carries you into neighboring B.C.

The Strawberry Triple Chair takes you to some first-rate novice terrain that cuts down through the lightly treed mid-mountain section. Farther to the right, the Standish Chair carries you to the top of Mount Standish and a mixture of runs from black diamond to easy greens that all wind back down to the village area.

On the backside of the Sunshine Day Lodge is the Wawa T-bar, which takes you to the top of some shorter but challenging intermediate runs that tend

**SKI NORQUAY—
FIVE 5-STAR FAVORITES**

Best Run for Vertical
Lone Pine

Best Overall Run
Excalibur

Best Restaurant
Joshua's

Best Nightclub/Bar
Wild Bill's

Best Accommodation
Mount Royal Hotel
Ken Fiske, Ski Norquay

to become filled with moguls as the traffic builds. But they are fun. The snow is less traveled than in some areas of the mountain, and while the T-bar may seem a bit of an antique, it's well placed, and the runs down are filled with surprises and some deep snow.

At the end of the day, downloading on the gondola to the Borgeau parking lot is one option, but the Borgeau Trail is a great laid-back way to take your final run. It's a gently sloping trail that carves a switchback route down to the parking lot.

HOW TO SKI SUNSHINE

Novices

You don't have to miss out on the view from the top of Lookout Mountain: there's a long, easy, gliding green run all the way down to the village. Just watch for the signs or you could find yourself in over your head. The Strawberry Triple Chair and the Assiniboine T-bar are also a good choice for a taste of some easy bowl-type skiing.

Intermediates

The Angel Express and the Great Divide chairs give you your best range of long giant slalom cruisers, along with some steep chutes, some delicious drop-offs, and the best of Sunshine's bowl skiing. The Wawa T-bar also has some good chutes, although they are a little narrow.

Experts

If you want the full extent of Sunshine's vertical, take the Angel Express to the Great Divide Triple to the top of the Lookout Mountain. From there Little Angel, Ecstasy and Big Angel offer some steep powder chute skiing. For some ultra-steep stuff, ski the runs off the Tee-Pee Town Chair, where the trees and the moguls add another dimension.

If you're planning to spend a week or more in Banff and want to ski all three mountains, it's worth considering linking up with the Club Ski program. A cooperative effort between the three resorts (Sunshine, Norquay and Skiing Louise), Club Ski is an informal guide and instruction program that puts skiers of similar ability together for a teaching tour of each resort. If you purchase lift tickets, there's no charge on the shuttle buses that run between all three resorts. Call 762-4561.

Visa, MC, Amex, T/CK

BANFF

WHERE TO STAY

The choice of accommodation in Banff is broad, to say the least. You can stay in the stately Banff Springs Hotel, with its legendary CP Hotel grandeur, or slum it in a main street motel with hot and cold running maids. You can isolate yourself at Sunshine Village, or be a heartbeat from the glitz of busy Banff Ave. Big rooms or small rooms; condos, timeshares, no-tell motels, period hotels, in town, out of town, on the edge of town . . .

Most accommodation can be booked through Banff Central Reservations at (403) 762-5561, toll-free (U.S. and Canada) 1-800-661-1676.

Expensive

Banff Park Lodge

A big, modern hotel in the middle of town, the Banff Park Lodge has over 200 rooms, some with fireplaces. It's glossy, efficient, somewhat soulless, but nonetheless a first-rate complex with amenities that include a swimming pool, whirlpool, steam room and shopping arcade. Rates $95–$200.

22 Lynx St. Tel (403) 762-4433, toll-free (U.S. & Canada) 1-800-661-9266

Visa, MC, Amex, Diners, enRoute, JCB, T/CK

Banff Springs Hotel

With the exception of the surrounding mountain peaks, there's no better-known landmark in Banff than the magnificent Banff Springs Hotel. Built in 1888, the Springs has undergone many renovations over the years, including the recent addition of a $55-million conference center. But the true magic of this Rocky Mountain castle remains its ageless elegance, which starts with the bell-person who parks your car and continues in every nook and cranny of the remarkable 850-room hotel. Among the facilities that this rambling edifice offers are 15 restaurants, indoor and outdoor pools, a health club complete with Nautilus equipment, saunas and hot tubs, a bowling alley, an 18-hole indoor miniature golf course, 40 shops and boutiques, and a grand ballroom capable of handling 1,600 people. Rooms range from small—some would say closet-size—doubles to one luxurious three-bedroom suite with its own lap pool. Even if you don't stay at the Springs, at least spend a couple of hours exploring. Rates $110–$800.

Spray Ave (1 mile/1.5 km outside of town). Tel (403) 762-2211

Visa, MC, Amex, Diners, enRoute, Discover, T/CK

Inns of Banff Park

The Inns of Banff Park has 180 large rooms and suites. They're all comfortable and well designed, but none have kitchen facilities. Amenities include a swimming pool, a superb restaurant, and a whirlpool and sauna. Rates $62–$160.

600 Banff Ave, on the edge of town. Tel (403) 762-4581, toll-free (U.S. & Canada) 1-800-661-1272

Visa, MC, Amex, enRoute, T/CK

Sunshine Village Inn

The only on-mountain accommodation available in Banff National Park, the Sunshine Inn is perfect for those who cherish quiet nights and early starts to the day's skiing. With just 84 rooms and limited facilities, this is not for the party and pampered crowd. You have to leave Banff when the last gondola goes up to the village, at 11 p.m. Still, the best nightlife show is the star-studded night sky. It's a special place. Rates $85–$145.

Tel (403) 762-6500, toll-free (U.S. & Canada) 1-800-661-1363

Visa, MC, Amex, T/CK

Moderate

The majority of Banff hotels and motels fall in the Moderate price range—that is, rooms run under $120, and package deals can bring that figure down to around $65. Here are the best.

Cascade Inn

Connected by tunnel to the Mount Royal Hotel, the Cascade was recently renovated to the tune of some $4 million. The Cascade has a great mid-town location close to the action. Rooms are large and beautifully decorated. The hallways are done up like turn-of-the-century railway cars. For something special, check in to the presidential suite with its glass-walled jacuzzi.

124 Banff Ave. Tel (403) 762-3311

Visa, MC, Amex, Diners, enRoute, JCB, T/CK

Charlton's Cedar Court

Sixty-five large rooms, some with fireplace and kitchen. Indoor swimming pool.

513 Banff Ave. Tel (403) 762-4485

Visa, MC, Amex, Diners, enRoute, T/CK

Charlton's Evergreen Court

Fifty-two large rooms, some with kitchens and some with separate bedrooms. Heated pool.

459 Banff Ave. Tel (403) 762-3307

Visa, MC, Amex, Diners, enRoute, T/CK

Douglas Fir Resort

Has 130 large rooms, plus several one- and two-bedroom suites, and some individual chalets. Facilities include indoor pool, water slide, squash and racquetball courts, and a grocery store.

On Tunnel Mountain Rd on the outskirts of town. Tel (403) 762-5591

Visa, MC, Amex, enRoute, T/CK

Mount Royal Hotel

For a great mid-town location, the Mount Royal is hard to beat. Recently renovated, the rooms are stylish and comfortable. There's a great little health club.

138 Banff Ave. Tel (403) 762-3331

Visa, MC, Amex, Diners, enRoute, JCB, T/CK

Inexpensive

For those on a budget or bent on a bargain, there are numerous low-end hotels and motels sprinkled throughout Banff. In most cases you won't pay more than $65 a night, and multi-day rates run even lower.

Traveller's Inn

Has 90 standard hotel rooms. Nothing fancy, but a few extras like sauna, hot tub and a breakfast restaurant.

401 Banff Ave. Tel (403) 762-4401

Visa, MC, Amex, T/CK

Two other options for the thrifty skier are the Banff International Hostel, which has room for 150 in four- to six-person bunk rooms (403-762-4122), and a growing number of bed & breakfast establishments (call Banff Bed & Breakfast Bureau at 403-762-5070).

WHERE TO EAT

Expensive

Giorgio's La Casa

First-rate Italian fare, including homemade pasta dishes and veal and seafood. Try the rabbit in green pepper and tomato sauce. The service is superb and the atmosphere—in three small rooms—decidedly romantic. Reservations recommended.

219 Banff Ave. Tel 762-5114

Visa, MC, Amex, T/CK

Le Beaujolais

Perhaps the swankiest restaurant in town, and certainly one of the most expensive. Primarily a French cuisine menu with a good selection of beef dishes, along with superb duck and veal. A stylish enclave with Belgian tapestries on the walls and a red rose on every table. Reservations recommended.

212 Buffalo St. Tel 762-2712

Visa, MC, Amex, T/CK

Rob Roy Dining Room

Your best choice for a dinner and dancing experience, the elegant Rob Roy features live entertainment for a swirl around the dance floor, and tableside preparation for your dining entertainment. Specialties include Alberta beef in all its varieties, plus game such as moose and buffalo. Wear your dancing shoes and your dress-up clothes. The view through the giant picture window is spectacular. Reservations recommended.

At the Banff Springs Hotel, Spray Ave. Tel 762-6842

Visa, MC, Amex, Diners, enRoute, T/CK

Ticino

Their Swiss-Italian menu features excellent schnitzel dishes as well as meat and chicken specialties. On the Italian side are fresh pastas and veal dishes. The decor of white stucco and wooden beams makes it less stuffy than others in this category. Reservations recommended.

205 Wolf St. Tel 762-3848

Visa, MC, Amex

Moderate

Bumper's

"If you haven't been to Bumper's, you haven't been to Banff" is the adage about this local favorite. And while that may simply be food for thought, one thing for sure is if you like your prime Alberta beef in large portions, Bumper's is your best bet. Try the awesome Man Mountain Cut, an 18-oz bludgeon of prime rib, or the extra-large ribs. The salad bar is equally awesome. No reservations needed, but hearty appetites are.

603 Banff Ave. Tel 762-2622

Visa, MC, Amex, Diners

The Caboose

The Caboose is a former baggage room in the Banff Via Rail station, and the ambience is all railroad, including the live sounds from passing freights. The menu features a handful of hearty staples, including prime rib, steak and lobster, king crab and rocky mountain trout. Casual and lively.

At the corner of Elk and Lynz streets. Tel 762-3622

Visa, MC, Amex, Diners, JCB, T/CK

Grizzly House

If fondue is your thing, the Grizzly has one for every palate, including rattlesnake, alligator and buffalo. In addition to the esoteric, you'll find more traditional cook-your-own choices such as cheese, meat and seafood—14 fondues in total. A place where two can dally whilst they dip.

207 Banff Ave. Tel 762-4055

Visa, MC, Amex, T/CK

Guido's

A casual Italian eatery with a wide assortment of fresh pasta dishes. The sourdough bread is excellent, and a particular favorite is the linguine with baby clams.

116 Banff Ave. Tel 762-4002

Visa, MC, Amex, T/CK

Magpie and Stump

The flavor of the Old West and a taste of Mexico is what you get at the Magpie, which features all the traditional Mexican favorites, including nachos, enchiladas, burritos and tacos. Also has a selection of gringo food such as steak, ribs and chicken. A fun place with live entertainment.

203 Caribou St. Tel 762-4067

Visa, MC, Amex, Diners, T/CK

Vault House

An Austrian-style eatery with the emphasis on schnitzels and fondues. A fun spot with live entertainment in the form of "happy Hans," a strolling, yodeling minstrel in lederhosen with a knack for getting everyone involved. Good fun, good food and good prices.

At the Banff Springs Hotel, Spray Ave. Tel 762-6879

Visa, MC, Amex

The Yard

A varied menu featuring Tex-Mex dishes plus seafood specialties.

Atop the King Edward Hotel on Banff Ave. Tel 762-5678

Visa, MC, Amex, JCB, T/CK

Inexpensive

Joe Btfsplk's Diner

A meat-and-potatoes menu that features real mashed potatoes and a great homemade meatloaf along with other old-time favorites. Also great homemade ice-cream, as well as a sublime bumbleberry pie.

221 Banff Ave. Tel 762-5529

Visa, MC, Amex, Diners, T/CK

Rose and Crown

Basic pub fare in a fun atmosphere. The fish and chips and bangers and mash are recommended, and you can wash them down with a choice from the extensive beer menu. Great nightly entertainment. Popular with locals.

202 Banff Ave. Tel 762-2121

Visa, MC, Amex, T/CK

Timberline Restaurant

Truck drivers, they say, know their pit stops, and the Timberline has been attracting road warriors for more than 30 years with its hearty, basic menu. Tourists also enjoy the spectacular view down the Bow valley corridor. The club sandwich with fresh turkey is a favorite, as is the Boston clam chowder.

Norquay Rd. Tel 762-2281

Visa, MC, Amex, T/CK

NIGHTLIFE

Whatever your choice of evening entertainment, the best way of getting from point A to point B is via the Happy Bus. This regular shuttle stops at, or close by, all the main action spots, and will drop you within stumbling distance of wherever you're staying. Stay away from your car if you're drinking: the RCMP spot checks in Banff are constant (and desirable). The Happy Bus is your best way to stay out of trouble.

Loud and Lively

Barbary Coast

A sports bar. The sporting memorabilia and live entertainment several decibels above conversation level make this a fun spot for the under-40 crowd. A great stand-up bar and room to dance as well. Do try the award-winning California cuisine.
119 Banff Ave. Tel 762-4616

Sidestreets

A little hard to spot despite its main street location, Sidestreets is fairly small, but its cheek-to-jowl ambience makes it popular with the crowd on the make.
319 Banff Ave. Tel 762-5004

Silver City Saloon

This is a Banff classic with its neo-American, Old Time western atmosphere and 44-ft bar. It's loud, smoky and frantic with live music. It's a basement location, which is just as well, because it's not the kind of place you'd like your mother to find you in—it's also called "Sin City" and "Sleazy City."
110 Banff Ave. Tel 762-3337

Whiskey Creek Saloon

The newest addition to the nightlife at the Springs, the saloon is huge, yet nearly always packed, probably because of the large-screen TVs, live entertainment, a giant dance floor and a crowd that loves to boogie. Lineups are common, but if you're a guest at the Springs your room key will usually get you a jump on the line.
In the Banff Springs Conference Centre. Tel 762-2211

Wild Bill's

Alberta may be cowboy country, but surprisingly Wild Bill's is the first genuine cowboy bar to hit town since the stagecoach was running, and it's my favorite new spot. It's named after Bill Peyto, one of the original park wardens and a bit of a wild man himself. The bar is huge, with room for 400 or so, features live music every night, has a dance floor for those inclined to two step (free instruction every Wednesday) and a decor that's all wood and stone, including a giant fireplace.

At the corner of Banff Ave and Caribou St.
Tel 762-0333

Mellow

Joshua's Pub

A small, cozy bar tucked away beside Joshua's restaurant, the pub has room only for about 35 people, but it's one of the few places in town where the hormone and music levels are less than frantic.
204 Caribou St. Tel 762-8010

DIVERSIONS

Ice Time

The Banff Recreation Centre has both public skating and public curling, which make a great change from the nightlife bustle. Rentals are available. On Mount Norquay Rd. Call 762-1235.

Hot Springs Eternal

Nothing takes the ache out of tired ski muscles than a comforting soak, and the Upper Hot Springs Pool is a must at least once during your trip to Banff. The water temperature averages around 100°F (38°C), and if you forget your bathing suit or towel, rentals are available. A massage service is also available. Hours: 12–9 weekdays, 8:30–11 weekends. Adults $3, children $1.50. On Mountain Ave. Tel 762-2056.

T/CK

For the Culture Vulture

In spite of Banff's good-time reputation, there are places for quieter moments. Check out the Natural History Museum at 112 Banff Ave (762-4747) or the Whyte Museum of the Canadian Rockies at 111 Bear St (762-2291). There are also regular live performances and films at the Banff Centre for the Performing Arts on St Julian Rd (762-6100).

LAKE LOUISE

HOW TO GET THERE

By Car: Lake Louise is 37 mi (60 km) west of Banff on Trans-Canada 1. It's about a 40-minute drive, and don't try to make it faster because the highway is riddled with RCMP radar traps. Another hazard motorists should be aware of is wandering wildlife. A full-size elk can do more damage than a half-ton truck.

By Bus: Brewster Transportation & Tours operates four daily shuttle runs from major Banff hotels to the Lake Louise ski area. From the village of Lake Louise, there's a regular, free shuttle service to the ski resort from four hotels—Château Lake Louise, Deer Lodge, Lake Louise Inn and Post Hotel.

If a panoramic view of blue-white glaciers and soaring peaks, wandering wildlife and the absence of glitzy resort trappings appeal to you, then Lake Louise is your ski town. Small, somewhat isolated—although the bright lights of Banff do beckon, just 40 minutes away—and bursting with some of the most majestic scenery anywhere in the world, Lake Louise is the epitome of a Rocky Mountain ski experience.

The village is tiny, with half a dozen hotels, a small mall, a train station and an RCMP detachment, and the Lake Louise ski area, the winter centerpiece of this dazzling wilderness tableau, is a skiing nirvana. First-time visitors might be excused for wondering what all the fuss is about when they take stock of the modest Whiskyjack base lodge area. But appearances are deceptive, and a glance at the trail map reveals the full extent of this vast Rocky Mountain giant. The sparsity of its base area creature comforts is attributed to the restrictions of ski operations imposed by the national park wherein it lies. To move a boulder or fell a tree requires specific permission, and although proposals for expanded facilities and on-slope accommodations are regularly presented, they are just as regularly rejected. But this bureaucratic tug-of-war does not in any way detract from the fine skiing.

Box 5
Lake Louise, Alberta
T0L 1E0
Tel (403) 522-3555

HOW TO GET THERE
By Car: The resort is a 10-minute drive from any of the hotels in Lake Louise. Follow the main road through the village, across the railway tracks and the Trans-Canada Highway, then take the Lake Louise Rd into the resort.

By Bus: Free shuttle buses leave regularly from all of the hotels.

THE SKIING

Skiing Louise—as the resort is officially called to distinguish it from the village and lake called Lake Louise—is arguably Canada's finest all-round ski area. It's definitely the largest, and for pure breathtaking scenery it is beyond compare. It is also a sprawling and diverse resort that for many is an intimidating array of four mountain faces and back bowls, two-thirds of which are found on the far side of the towering 8,650-ft (2636-m) summit.

Two mountains actually make up the Skiing Louise ski area—Whitehorn and Lipalian—and it's the scope of the skiing at Skiing Louise that is the true measure of its appeal. The boundary lines of the resort encompass more than 4,000 acres (1600 ha) of varied skiing ranging from top to bottom beginner runs to unparalleled and untracked bowl skiing that keeps even the most jaded powder hounds happy. The snow falls regularly and often, bringing an annual average of about 140 in (355 cm). In the back bowls that figure is often surpassed, while on the more exposed south side, snowmaking guns cover more than 1,600 acres (640 ha) to augment the natural fall.

All told, 50 marked trails cascade down the four mountain faces, with eight lifts capable of spreading 21,500 skiers an hour across the broad expanse of the resort. It's easy to be daunted by the vastness of the terrain, but even novices or modest intermediates can gain a full measure of the Louise experience because each chairlift services at least one green or beginner's run. And that's good, because even if the skiing proves to be more than you can handle, the 360-degree vista from the summit yields a mountain panorama unsurpassed in all of Canada, with more than a dozen peaks topping the 10,000-ft (3050-m) mark. Even if your legs

Base Elevation:
5,393 ft (1644 m)

Summit Elevation:
8,650 ft (2636 m)

Vertical Drop:
3,257 ft (994 m)

Skiable Terrain:
4,000 acres (1600 ha)

Number of Trails: 50

Longest Run: 5 mi (8 km)

Lifts & Capacity: 3 quads,
2 triples, 3 doubles, T-bar,
platter; 21,500 skiers per
hour

Daily Lift Ticket: $38
Weekly: $172 (5 days)

Annual Snowfall:
140 in (355 cm)

No. Days Skiing 91–92: 180

Snowmaking: Front side,
1,600 acres (640 ha)

Terrain Mix:
N 25%, I 45%, E 30%

Snow Phone: 244-6665

survive the endless descents, the rubber-necking that occurs as you try to drink in all that scenery will surely take its toll.

Unless you're a regular at Skiing Louise, it's best to tackle the skiing in stages best suited to your ability. Once you get a feel for the layout, you can experiment. The south side, or the front face of Skiing Louise, has a good mixture of the long and winding and the steep and fast, including the men's and women's World Cup downhill runs, a pair of devilishly fast full-bore cruisers. The Larch area on the backside has an equally good mixture of the tame and the testy, but avoid skiing this area on crowded days, especially after lunch.

But it's the back bowls that give you the most value for your money at Skiing Louise. Accessible via the south-side lifts, then from the Paradise Chair, runs like Shoulder Roll, Brown Shirt and Whitehorn One are long, wide-open, above-treeline freefalls that aggressive intermediates and experts will relish. Novices, too, can sample the Larch area; Saddleback, Pika and Pika Connector carry you smoothly and safely back down to the Temple Lodge.

HOW TO SKI SKIING LOUISE
Novices

Start on Wiwaxy to get comfortable and then, for a visit to the Larch area and Temple Lodge, take Saddleback and Pika. Ski Lookout on Larch and return to the base via Eagle Meadows and Wiwaxy.

Intermediates

Intermediates can ski almost anywhere on Louise, but for the best long run don't miss Meadowlark. For a taste of powder in a wide bowl run, check out Boomerang.

Experts

Ski the Summit Platter and Paradise Chair for the best combination of lifts. From there you'll just love runs like Outer Limits, Whitehorn One and Flight Chutes. Shoulder Roll and Pika are your full-bore cruising choices, and for full-on vertical try the Ridge Run. High Saddleback is a great powder chute, and the Rock Garden, an unmarked run off to the left of the Larch Chair, is worth a visit.

SKI WITH A FRIEND

When they tell you to ski with a friend at Skiing Louise, they're not suggesting it for companionship or safety, but rather to give you a full exposure to the terrain of Lake Louise. "Ski Friends" are volunteer hosts and hostesses who will give you a free guided tour of the ski terrain. It's a great way to discover parts of the mountain that you might never stumble across in a month of skiing. Tours leave from the base lodge at different times during the day.

WHERE TO STAY

Expensive

Château Lake Louise

Everything about the magnificent Château reeks of style—and money. And the recent $65-million facelift just adds to the luster. Make no mistake, this is one fantastic place to stay, and if you have money in your budget for only one night of supreme indulgence, experience this Rocky Mountain castle. There are 515 rooms—some are two-bedroom suites—plus facilities that include a recreation center, indoor pool, three dining rooms, two bars and about 30 shops and boutiques. Outside you can skate on Lake Louise or take horse-drawn sleigh rides. Rates $95–$725 (for a suite with all the trimmings). Watch for their ski packages.

Tel (403) 522-3511
Visa, MC, Amex, Diners, enRoute, Discover, JCB, T/CK

Emerald Lake Lodge
About a 30-minute drive from Lake Louise in Yoho National Park, the lodge
has 85 units, each with a fireplace and a balcony overlooking the frozen
waters of its namesake. It's isolated but spectacularly beautiful, and well worth
the extra drive if you crave scenic isolation. Also has saunas and a giant
outdoor hot tub. Rates $110–$260. From the Trans-Canada Highway turn
right onto Emerald Lake Rd.
Tel (604) 343-6321, toll-free (U.S. & Canada) 1-800-663-6336
Visa, MC, Amex, T/CK

Post Hotel
If I truly have a favorite place to stay in Lake Louise, it's the Post Hotel.
Owned and operated by André and George Schwartz, this delightful 95-room
lodge along the shores of the Pipestone River is the embodiment of the Lake
Louise alpine spirit. Although the original and somewhat modest Post has
undergone a $15-million refurbishment, none of the European style and
warmth has been sacrificed. Luxuries include an indoor pool and steam bath,
plus one of the best dining rooms (see Where to Eat) in the Rocky Mountains.
Rates $160–$255 (for a riverbank cabin). A three-day ski package is available.
Tel (403) 522-3989, toll-free (U.S. & Canada) 1-800-661-1586
Visa, MC, Amex, T/CK

Moderate
Deer Lodge
In the shadow of all those towering peaks, Deer Lodge is a reasonable and
moderately priced option. Comfortable and friendly, with rooms that are small
but functional, it's a typical rustic mountain lodge, with not too many frills but
a lot of warm feelings. Rates $65–$125.
Tel (403) 522-3747, toll-free (Canada & U.S.) 1-800-661-1595
Visa, MC, Amex, enRoute

Lake Louise Inn
A more recent addition to the Lake Louise landscape, the Inn is a neat and tidy
collection of condo and motel units. Efficient and convenient, the Inn is

definitely more suited to young families, where child-proof utility is more important than the style of the room-service waiter. Facilities include a pool, saunas and steam rooms. Rates $75–$175 (for a multi-bedroom unit).
Tel (403) 522-3791, toll-free (western Canada & U.S.) 1-800-661-1586
Visa, MC, Amex, Diners, enRoute

Inexpensive
West Louise Lodge
Because of the limitations on development in Lake Louise, inexpensive accommodation lies farther afield. To be precise, in Field, B.C., sometimes called Lake Louise West, and the place where locals head on Sundays to take advantage of B.C.'s more lenient liquor laws. About a 15-minute drive from Lake Louise, West Louise Lodge is your economic alternative. The hotel has 44 basic rooms, and it's a popular place with students and long-duration visitors. Rates start at $43.
Tel (604) 343-6311
Visa, MC, Amex, enRoute, T/CK

WHERE TO EAT
There's not a lot of choice in Lake Louise. The major hotels all have dining rooms and less formal restaurants, but after that your choice is bar chow at the various watering holes (also in the hotels) or a quick snack from the deli, bake shop or convenience store in the Samson Mall. But don't despair, the formal fare is excellent at both the Post and the Château, and keep in mind that Banff is a reasonable distance for a dinner drive.

(If you have a room with a kitchen, stock up on groceries at Safeway in Banff, or better still in Calgary, because selection is definitely limited in Lake Louise.)

A Note on Breakfast and Lunch
Breakfast is best taken at your hotel. All offer everything from buffet spreads to elegant room service. In fact, consider ordering breakfast room service if you're staying at either the Château or the Post. It's a little indulgence that adds about $10 to the average breakfast for two, but the sheer decadence of munching on English muffins, sipping fresh orange juice and idly gazing out the window at one of the most awesome mountain tableaus on earth is truly a state of bliss. If on the other hand you just can't stand not being the first on the lifts, you can grab some

exotic muffins and pastries, plus excellent java-jolt cappuccino and espresso, at the coffee bar on the ground floor of the Whiskyjack base lodge. Try a Lake Louise favorite, Mocha—it's half coffee and half hot chocolate.

Your mid-day break is best taken on the mountain, especially if the weather is sunny. Bring your own if you prefer; Lake Louise does not sneer at brown-baggers, and the three on-mountain lodges have extensive decks and bring-your-own sections. The mountain fare is good, ranging from hearty stews, chilies, daily specials and monster sandwiches. On sunny days, burgers are barbecued on the deck at the Temple Lodge.

Expensive

The Edelweiss Dining Room

The Château's other formal dining room is smaller (by about half) than the Victoria, but the vaulted ceilings and wall tapestries provide a regal setting. Game is the specialty here—buffalo, moose, duck—along with more traditional fare.

In the Château Lake Louise. Tel 522-3511

Visa, MC, Amex, Diners, enRoute, Discover, T/CK

Post Hotel Dining Room

The gracious and congenial host-operators of the Post, brothers André and George Schwartz, acquired their reputation as purveyors of fine dining honestly—as proprietors of several noteworthy dining spots in Banff. Now that they are focusing all their expertise on the Post, its dining room has a well-deserved reputation as one of the best in the region. It features elegant and attentive European service and a continental menu that includes fresh game. You won't be disappointed, and if your budget can handle only one evening of sumptuous dining, make your reservation at the Post.

In the Post Hotel. Tel 522-3989

Victoria Dining Room

With its marvelously baroque setting complete with wood paneling, period paintings, log fires and spectacular picture windows, it's often easy to overlook the food in the Château's main dining room. And while the food is generally not at the leading edge of the dining experience, it is very good, with a wide

selection of meat, fowl and seafood. Impeccable service and an elegant turn-of-the-century atmosphere. Reservations recommended.
In the Château Lake Louise. Tel 522-3511
Visa, MC, Amex, Diners, enRoute, Discover, JCB, T/CK

Moderate
Café Louise
A casual family-style hotel restaurant. Good basic chicken and Alberta beef dishes.
In Deer Lodge. Tel 522-3747
No cards

Heritage Restaurant
Nothing fancy here, just solid family food, with an emphasis on meat and potatoes and pasta dishes. Casual and convenient if you have youngsters to think about.
In the Lake Louise Inn. Tel 522-3791
Visa, MC, Amex, Diners, enRoute

Walliser Stube Wine Bar
For me, fondues are the quintessential ski vacation meal. And few places do it better than this cozy little (70 seats) wine bar. Cheese, meat, seafood, fruit—just about anything you can cook in a pot is available. It's fun, informal and certainly affordable.
In the Château Lake Louise. Tel 522-3511
Visa, MC, Amex, Diners, enRoute, Discover, T/CK

NIGHTLIFE
The best nightlife in Lake Louise is the inky stillness that yields a clear sky studded with stars and dancing with northern lights. This is definitely nature's show, and quiet walks on the edge of the wilderness, a few midnight twirls around the skating rink, or a chance encounter with a wandering moose or sheep can leave you as breathless as the most pounding discotheque.

Not that you can't rock the rafters in the Château's Glacier Lounge or Charlie Two's over at the Lake Louise Inn, or settle down for some après-dinner drinks and entertainment in a small assortment of other watering holes. But the restless and relentless nightlife hound is much better off in Banff.

LAKE LOUISE—USEFUL
TELEPHONE NUMBERS
(area code 403)

RCMP 522-3811

Medical Clinic 522-2184

Brewster Transportation and
Tours 522-3544

Greyhound Bus Lines
522-3574

Taxi and Tours Lake Louise
522-2020

Hertz Rent-a-Car 522-3969

DIVERSIONS

Kingmik Expeditions Dog Sled Tours

For a truly novel experience in the Lake Louise area, try dog-sledding with Kingmik Expeditions. You can take short half-hour tours or half-day and full-day excursions. Owner-operator Doug Hanna has 110 dogs and sleds of various sizes. The tours take place in the spectacular Blae Berry valley, 12 mi (19 km) north of Golden, B.C., and about 45 minutes west of Lake Louise off Hwy 1.

Also available are overnight trips, and for a true mountain experience you can stay overnight at the Goat Mountain Lodge. You can even drive your own teams if so inclined. Half-hour tours cost $23 an adult, $15 for children. For a half-day it's $85 per adult, and a full day is $125. Doug will meet you in either Lake Louise or Golden.
Tel 522-3525. No cards.

Skating on Lake Louise

Even if you've never laced on a pair of skates, there's no place on earth more suited to skating than Lake Louise—the lake, that is. With an almost surreal setting, the cleared rink in the embrace of the Château's facade is the best outdoor skating rink in the world. Bring your blades (or rent them at the rink), and if you can't remember the last time you played pick-up pond hockey, you'll love the impromptu games that get started. This is magic on ice, and a memorable vignette from anyone's Lake Louise experience.

Skoki Lodge

There's no shortage of cross-country ski trails in and around Lake Louise, but for a unique back country experience, Skoki Lodge, 7 mi (11 km) up the Skoki valley from Lake Louise, is hard to beat. Built in

1930 for a group of alpine adventurers, the main lodge and three adjacent cabins are comfortable burnished log structures with room for just 22 guests. There's only one way in, and that's on skis, either cross-country or telemark, and then it's old-fashioned high-alpine hospitality. Guests can explore the mountain ridges and adjacent valleys, replenish their energy with sumptuous meals, and relax in the glow of wood fires in rugged stone fireplaces. Rate is $93 a night including meals. Discounts for multi-night stays.

Tel 522-3555

Visa, MC, Amex, CK, T/CK

JASPER

Jasper and its ski resort of Marmot Basin are 580 mi (362 km) west of Edmonton, 250 mi (400 km) northwest of Calgary. Edmonton and Calgary airports are served by major airlines, with connections from major centers.

By Car: From Calgary follow Trans-Canada 1 to Banff, then north to Lake Louise. In Lake Louise pick up Hwy 93 north (also known as the Icefields Parkway) all the way to Jasper. The drive takes about 4 1/2 hours, and the scenery is spectacular.

From Edmonton, take Hwy 16 west. Count on 3 1/2 hours.

By Bus: Greyhound Bus Lines runs four Edmonton–Jasper round trips daily. From Calgary, Brewster Gray Lines runs a daily round trip.

By Train: Via Rail operates service to Jasper on an irregular schedule. Tel 1-800-561-8630 (toll-free western Canada)

Some people suggest that Jasper, a beautiful town of 4,500 right in the middle of the largest national park in Alberta, is just like Banff used to be 25 years ago. What they refer to is its size and relatively undeveloped state. That may be part of the reason Jasper is so often overshadowed by its bigger neighbor, especially when it comes to skiing. But its charm should not be underestimated—and neither should the skiing at Marmot Basin, 14 mi (22 km) away.

Nestled in the middle of the 4,135 sq mi (10 880 km^2) Jasper National Park, Jasper began as a resting spot for traveling trappers, grew during the glory days of trains, and is now a historic tourist site that draws 2 million visitors a year. Remarkably, it has remained in perfect harmony with its majestic mountain setting. Jasper has always held a special place in my heart, for the easygoing nature of the locals, the unhurried pace and the sense of being in a very special place untouched by the pressures and problems of the world outside. And that's important to know, because you'll be staying here—Marmot does not have on-site accommodation.

The peaks, the glaciers, the high alpine valleys all form an amphitheatre for the rest of Jasper's natural wonders. Waterfalls and whitewater rivers, canyons scoured from the landscape by glaciers 60 million years ago, and wildlife abundant and unperturbed by humans are all part of the magnificent natural tapestry.

The accoutrements are satisfying also, with easy elegance available at the Jasper Park Lodge or some down-home foot-stomping to live bands at the Athabasca Hotel.

MARMOT BASIN

Box 1300
Jasper, Alberta
T0E 1E0
Tel (403) 852-3816

HOW TO GET THERE

By Car: Marmot Basin is 12 mi (19 km) south of Jasper, about 20 minutes along Hwy 93 to the Marmot Sideroad.

By Bus: Regular shuttle buses (Brewster Transportation and Tours) depart from the major Jasper hotels and return from Marmot between 3:15 and 5:30 p.m. Don't miss the last one—it's an expensive taxi ride home.

THE SKIING

Although not as big as Skiing Louise nor as high as Sunshine, Marmot Basin deserves no inferiority complex, for it is an excellent all-round mountain, with fine snow and uncrowded slopes. It may lack a touch of vertical, but it makes up for it with otherwise superb skiing.

Marmot encompasses 850 acres (340 ha) of ski terrain, with 2,300 ft (700 m) of lift-serviced vertical and another 500 ft (152 m) of pitch available to those who care to climb. There's a mix of below- and above-treeline slopes, some wide bowls and glade runs, and some steep pitches, headwalls and powder chutes off the top of the Knob Chair. Overall this is an excellent mountain for high-speed giant slalom cruising, but with enough options to keep you exploring for a week. Fifty-two trails is the official count, but Marmot is the kind of place where exploring is encouraged by the very nature of its loose, sprawling layout.

The location of the Paradise Chalet at mid-mountain makes this an easy area for groups of varying ability to meet up regularly, with the lower treed runs supplying most of the easy cruising slopes and the upper half of the mountain the more demanding options. The Knob Chair carries better skiers to the summit ridge, where the steep powder is most often found, and from there many opt for the 500-ft (152-m) slog to the Marmot peak and the full-tilt vertical that the Peak Run provides.

HOW TO SKI MARMOT

Novices

Stick to the Eagle Express, Triple and Caribou lifts. A favorite of the easy-cruising set is Old Road, off either the Express or Yellow chairlifts.

MARMOT BASIN—STATISTICALLY SPEAKING

Base Elevation:
5,640 ft (1720 m)

Summit Elevation:
7,940 ft (2420 m)

Vertical Drop:
2,300 ft (700 m)

Skiable Terrain:
850 acres (340 ha)

Number of Trails: 52

Longest Run: 3.5 mi (5.5 km)

Lifts & Capacity: 1 quad,
1 triple, 3 doubles, 2 T-bars;
10,080 skiers per hour

Daily Lift Ticket: $33
Weekly: $149

Annual Snowfall:
186 in (472 cm)

No. Days Skiing 91–92: 150

Snowmaking: Limited

Terrain Mix:
N 35%, I 35%, E 30%

Snow Phone: 488-5909

Intermediates

There's a great mixture of runs off the Eagle Express, Triple, Caribou and Yellow chairlifts.

Experts

Take the Eagle Express to the triple chair and ski the black diamond runs off the Triple or Knob chairlifts. You can also traverse to the Eagle Ridge area for some of the best glade skiing in the west.

WHERE TO STAY

Jasper has a good choice of accommodations across the price spectrum, and many feature special three-day rates.

All can be booked through Ski World at (403) 852-4242.

Expensive

Charlton's Château Jasper

The Château has 120 luxury rooms and suites, and some super-large suites come complete with large jacuzzis and a bar. Facilities include a fine dining room, piano bar, indoor pool with sauna and hot tubs, and underground parking. Rates $80–$195.
96 Geikie St. Tel (403) 852-5644
Visa, MC, Amex, Diners, enRoute, JCB

Jasper Inn

The Jasper Inn features a combination of hotel-style rooms and 141 chalet-style condominiums, most with kitchen and fireplace. Some of the two-bedroom suites have jacuzzis. Amenities include an indoor pool, sauna, steam room, whirlpool and ski waxing room. Rates $65–$125.
98 Geikie St. Tel (403) 852-4461, toll-free (western Canada) 1-800-661-1933
Visa, MC, Amex, Diners, enRoute, Discover

Jasper Park Lodge
Set amidst 1,000 acres (400 ha) of wilderness, the Lodge is a collection of log buildings, chalets and cabins on the shore of Lac Beauvert, just five minutes from the Jasper townsite. There's a total of 437 rooms, including suites, some in individual log cabins, and many with fireplace and jacuzzi. There are four dining rooms, a nightclub, lounge, heated outdoor pool, health club and shopping concourse. Outdoor options include cross-country skiing, skating, sleigh rides and snowshoeing. Ski package prices start at about $208 per room double occupancy and include lift ticket, breakfast and one dinner. Individual room rates start at $87.
On Lodge Rd. Tel (403) 852-3301
Visa, MC, Amex, Diners, enRoute, Discover, JCB

Moderate
Lobstick Lodge
A good family hotel with oversize rooms, some with kitchenettes. Amenities include an indoor pool, two jacuzzis, hot tub, sauna, steam room and laundry facilities. Rates $55–$95.
Tel (403) 852-4431
Visa, MC, Amex, Diners, enRoute

Marmot Lodge
Large, bright rooms with some designer touches. Many units have full kitchens and fireplaces. Facilities include indoor pool, jacuzzi, sauna, laundry and pay-TV movies. Rates $65–$115.
Tel (403) 852-4471
Visa, MC, Amex, Diners, JCB, T/CK

Pyramid Lake Bungalows
Has main lodge with 42 units, plus four eight-plex chalet-style units. Room amenities include kitchens, fireplaces and whirlpools. Duplexes can accommodate up to six people. Ideal for families. Rates $55–$75.
About 3 mi (5 km) northwest of Jasper townsite on the shores of Pyramid Lake, on Pyramid Lake Rd. Tel (403) 852-3536
Visa, MC, T/CK

Sawridge Hotel
Has 154 large rooms with two queen beds, but no kitchen units. Facilities include indoor pool, jacuzzi, sauna, two outdoor hot tubs, and a nightclub, coffee shop and dining room. Rates $94–$114.
Tel (403) 852-5111
Visa, MC, Amex, enRoute, T/CK

Inexpensive
Astoria Hotel
An unpretentious mid-town hotel with comfortable rooms and a few trimmings like mini-fridges and TVs. Rates $48–$60.
404 Connaught Dr. Tel (403) 852-3351
Visa, MC, Amex, enRoute, T/CK

Athabasca Hotel
The Atha' B, as it's known, it a turn-of-the-century main street hotel right in the center of Jasper. It's not fancy, but it was recently refurbished, and the rooms, while small, are comfortable. Rates $40–$55.
510 Patricia St. Tel (403) 852-3386
Visa, MC, Amex, Diners, T/CK

WHERE TO EAT
Expensive
Cavell Room
The premier dining room in the Jasper Park Lodge, it features a wide-ranging menu that includes beef dishes, seafood and other specialties. If you want to drop a bundle, and get the service and attention that goes with it, this is your choice.
In the Jasper Park Lodge. Tel 852-3301
Visa, MC, Amex, enRoute, JCB, T/CK

Moderate
Beauvert Room
Stylish service, great atmosphere and a varied menu featuring everything from fresh fish to Alberta beef. Also has a great view over Lac Beauvert.
In the Jasper Park Lodge. Tel 852-3301
Visa, MC, Amex, enRoute, JCB, T/CK

Tokyo Tom's
My favorite in Jasper. Rumor has it that Tom used to drive the fresh sushi in from the West Coast. He may not do that now, but Tokyo Tom's is still a great place for Japanese fare such as sushi, tempura and shabu shabu. The atmosphere is casual, the saki flows liberally, and the fish is still the freshest east of Vancouver.
410 Connaught Dr. Tel 852-3780
Visa, MC, Amex, Diners

Tonquin Prime Rib
If prime rib is your passion, few places do it better than the Tonquin. Large, perfectly prepared portions of Alberta beef with all the trimmings.
In the Tonquin Motor Inn, 100 Connaught Dr. Tel 852-4966
Visa, MC, Amex, Diners, enRoute, T/CK

Inexpensive
Echoes
A bright, stylish dining room with a menu that ranges from prime rib to specialty seafoods.
In the Marmot Lodge. Tel 852-4471
Visa, MC, Amex, Diners, JCB

Jasper Pizza Place
The best pizza in town, along with other specialty items. The Caesar salad and the French onion soup are both good deals.
402 Connaught Dr, next door to the Astoria Hotel. Tel 852-3225
Visa, Amex, T/CK

L&W Family Restaurant
Good basic grub such as burgers, ribs, BBQ chicken and Greek specialties. Fast and friendly, with a pleasant atrium-like setting.
Corner of Hazel and Patricia streets. Tel 852-4114
Visa, MC, Amex, Diners, T/CK

Papa George's Restaurant

Papa's is a local favorite that has been around since 1925. Hearty portions of such staples as pasta, chicken and burgers, along with some interesting vegetarian dishes.

In the Astoria Hotel, 404 Connaught Dr. Tel 852-3351

Visa, MC, Amex, T/CK

Something Else

With a name like that, you'd expect it to be. And it is, at least when it comes to the variety. Good Cajun and Greek dishes, as well as fresh semolina pastas and stir-frys. A local favorite.

621 Patricia St. Tel 852-3850

Visa, MC, Amex, enRoute

NIGHTLIFE

Loud and Lively

Astoria Bar

Definitely the place to go on Friday night for the legendary happy hour. Make sure you get there by 5:30 or you won't get in. Lots of libations, happy après-skiers, occasional live entertainment and impromptu dancing.

In the Astoria Hotel, 404 Connaught Dr. Tel 852-3351

Champs

A loud and glitzy disco with a DJ spinning out the sounds with an accompanying light show. A good place for dancing, and if that's not your speed but you like the music, it also has a pool table.

In the Sawridge Hotel. Tel 852-5111

Dead Animal Room

A somewhat gruesome appellation for what is more formally known as the Trophy Room. If you can stand the wildlife staring down at you from the walls, this is the place to go for dancing and down-home good times. Has live entertainment three or four nights a week, along with a pool table, darts and lots of mingling.

In the Athabasca Hotel, 510 Patricia St. Tel 852-3386

Tent City

Another place popular with the dancing crowd, with its DJ and up-town music. Doesn't get rocking until later in the evening, but then it's non-stop.

In the Jasper Park Lodge. Tel 852-3301

Mellow

Nick's

A piano bar environment, with a pianist occasionally tickling the ivories, and mellow music from a great sound system the rest of the time. A pleasant atrium setting.

In the Tonquin Motor Inn. Tel 852-4966

O'Sheas

A sports bar that is surprisingly low-key. Has multiple TVs for the jocks, a cozy fireplace for the romantics. An odd combination, but it works as a place to relax.

In the Athabasca Hotel, 510 Patricia St. Tel 852-3386

DIVERSIONS

Give Yourself the Edge

Given the price of skis these days it's prudent to try before you buy, and Edge Control, a rental and tuning specialty shop, features an impressive lineup of high-end rental skis. Also has more mainstream rentals and the largest selection of rental snowboards in town, along with snowshoes. You won't find a more accommodating and knowledgeable group of ski technicians anywhere in the Rockies. Tell them what you're looking for in a ski, and they'll put you on a pair to match your ability and pocketbook. If you're content with your current skis but feel they need a little tune-up, the boys will do a bang-up job of tailoring them to your taste. Just drop them off at the end of the day and they'll be tuned and waxed in time for an early morning pickup the next day. Ask for Blair, and he'll give you the straight goods. 604 Patricia St. Call 852-4945.

Winter Wonderland

If sightseeing is on your list of things to do in Jasper, don't miss the Athabasca Falls, a stunning display of rainbow-hued spray and dazzling ice formations. Take Hwy 93 south of Jasper for about 18 mi (30 km).

Crawl the Canyons

For something totally off the wall, I highly recommend taking a half-day to explore the frozen waterfalls, ice caves and underground rivers at Maligne Canyon. Guides run two tours a day (9 a.m. and 1 p.m.), with bus pickup at your hotel and suitable footwear part of the package. Call 852-3370.

Aquatic Antics

For a warmer diversion, the Jasper Aquatic Centre is a great place to dive in to with its full-size pool, 180-ft (55-m) waterslide, jacuzzis and steam room. Next door is the Jasper Activity Centre, with a skating rink, racquetball courts, weight room and curling sheets. 401 Pyramid Lake Rd. Call 852-3381 or 852-3663.

KANANASKIS

HOW TO GET THERE

By Plane: The Kananaskis region is approximately 45 mi (72 km) from Calgary. Calgary International Airport is served by most major carriers with connections from all major North American cities.

By Car: The Kananaskis region is about an hour's drive from Calgary. Take Trans-Canada 1 west towards Banff, and turn south on the Kananaskis Trail (Hwy 40).

By Bus: Brewster Transportation and Tours runs a shuttle service from Calgary to Banff, with a stop-off at the Kananaskis turn-off for a connecting shuttle service into the ski area. The bus also stops in Canmore.

The Kananaskis region encompasses more than 1520 sq mi (4000 km^2) of picturesque wilderness along the eastern slope of the Rocky Mountains. Starting approximately 25 mi (40 km) southwest of Calgary the region runs west to the boundary of Banff National Park. Three provincial parks—Bragg Creek, Bow Valley and Peter Lougheed—have been created within the region, along with two ski resorts. The best known of the two resorts is Nakiska at Mount Allan, the state-of-the-art resort designed and built for the alpine events of the 1988 Winter Olympic Games.

Box 1988
Kananaskis Village, Alberta
T0L 2H0
Tel (403) 591-7777

HOW TO GET THERE

By Plane: Nakiska and the nearby resort village of Kananaskis are 62 mi (100 km) southwest of Calgary. Calgary International Airport is served by major airlines, with connections from major centers.

By Car: Nakiska and Kananaskis Village are about an hour's drive from Calgary and about a 45-minute drive from Banff. Take Trans-Canada 1 west from Calgary (or east from Banff) to Hwy 40 and turn south. Nakiska is about 2.5 mi (4 km) from the Kananaskis resort village.

By Bus: Brewster Transportation and Tours has a shuttle service from the airport and downtown Calgary that stops en route to Banff. Brewster also operates a free shuttle bus between the ski area and Kananaskis Village.

So let's get it straight. Nakiska is the ski area. It's on Mount Allan. The resort village is Kananaskis. Together they make up the resort of Nakiska at Mount Allan in Kananaskis.

Alberta's newest ski resort was built for the alpine skiing events at the 1988 Winter Olympics in an area that most experts agree is not ideal for a ski resort of any kind. The major reason is snow—not so much the lack of it, because Nakiska annually receives about the same as Lake Louise, but keeping it. The warm chinook winds that blast out of the lowlands to the south have an annoying habit of reducing a few feet of snow to an inch or so of sludge overnight. To counter this, the most expensive and sophisticated snowmaking system in the world was built. The network of pumps, compressors, snow guns and pipes cost more than $5 million to install, draws millions of gallons of water a day from the Kananaskis River and covers virtually every square foot of slope with snow. It's expensive and wildly impractical, but it does work to an extent.

The nearby resort village is a brand-new collection of three hotels, a recreation center and assorted amenities. It's not the liveliest spot in the Rockies, but it does have a certain cachet that brand spanking new facilities produce. It's also the closest resort to Calgary, and the accommodation is one of the best bargains around. In an ongoing effort to attract skiers, the three hotels offer some astonishingly low package deals, much to the chagrin of operators in nearby Banff, who take exception to tax dollars—with which the resort was built—providing subsidized competition. Still, it's the skier who benefits, and with the nearby Olympic mountain as a partner, it's a combination that's hard to ignore.

Base Elevation:
5,033 ft (1525 m)

Summit Elevation:
7,460 ft (2260 m)

Vertical Drop:
3,012 ft (920 m)

Skiable Terrain:
230 acres (92 ha)

Number of Trails: 30

Longest Run: 2 mi (3.2 km)

Lifts & Capacity: 2 quads,
1 triple, 1 double, 1 surface;
8,620 skiers per hour

Annual Snowfall:
80 in (200 cm)

No. Days Skiing 91–92: 130

Snowmaking: 80%

Terrain Mix:
N 16%, I 70%, E 14%

Snow Phone: 235-9191

THE SKIING

A look at the trail map of Nakiska tells you that there's not much danger of getting lost or stumbling on trails that are a cut above your ability level. It's so straightforward in its design that it's almost as if it came from a computer given instructions to put all the tough stuff at the top, fill the middle with intermediate runs and leave the bottom for the novices.

In fact, Nakiska was designed with all the latest computer assisted design techniques, and produced by Ecosign of Whistler, the same company that created the long, wide fall-line runs of Blackcomb.

The eastern slopes of Mount Allan serve up steep, challenging chutes from the summit down to mid-mountain, where you can pick up one of a dozen winding trails back down to the base lodge. In short, a mountain made for the neat and tidy among us.

Three lifts do it all, with the Olympic Quad chair zooming you to mid-mountain and a connection to the Gold Chair, which deposits you at the summit, about 400 yd (360 m) below the start of the men's Olympic downhill course. It's simple, basic and, well, just a touch boring. Not that you can't get your adrenaline rush from the black diamond chutes, but it seems there's something missing.

And there is. Something called powder snow. Nakiska's man-made product just isn't like the real stuff. It's what westerners laughingly call "eastern powder," a dense, hard-packed highway of white that demands sharp edges and shock absorbers for knees. That's what man-made snow produces: a dense, hard skiing surface that is tailor-made for a downhill race course, but not exactly what recreational skiers have come to expect in western Canada. The advantage though is that in relatively poor natural snow years the Nakiska system can still produce a durable coverage that the other Alberta resorts just can't match.

Still, the vertical at just a touch over 3,000 ft (920 m) is what gives Nakiska its punch. The upper part of the mountain's 230 acres (92 ha) is steep and demanding terrain with a variety of chutes, drop-offs and tricky little pitches. The bumps tend to grow large up there as well, and you can get a good mix of fall-line moguls, some stand-on-your-head vertical and an all-out 2-mi-long (3.2-km) top to bottom dose of giant slalom cruising.

As Canada's newest resort, Nakiska's greatest attributes may be the state-of-the-art design and development, which produced superbly laid-out trails, and the support technology that provides the most consistent snow coverage and trail grooming found anywhere in western Canada. It's a mountain made for the 90s, and with 70 percent of its terrain in that intermediate comfort zone, it's a mountain that most of us will be comfortable skiing.

HOW TO SKI NAKISKA
Novices
Stick to the Bronze Chair on the lower mountain, where there are half a dozen easy trails. If you're feeling ambitious, take the Olympic Chair and pick up the long, winding intermediate run to your left.

Intermediates
The Silver Chair takes you to some solid intermediate runs that have some good pitch but are a tad short. Steer clear of the black diamond run that parallels the area's boundary lines. The Olympic Chair gives you access to some longer runs, but the variety is limited.

Experts
Only one place to go for vertical, and that's the top third of the mountain. About a dozen black diamond chutes can be picked up off the Gold Chair. They are short, though, so you might want to extend them by taking a fast giant slalom cruising route back down to the base of the Olympic Chair.

WHERE TO STAY
Moderate
Hotel Kananaskis
More intimate than the Lodge, the hotel has 69 rooms and suites, all done up

in style. Rooms feature king-size beds and mini-bars, while the suites include fireplace, jacuzzi and loft sleeping. The hotel also has a small health club, but you can use all the facilities at the adjacent Lodge. Rates $80–$120.
Tel (403) 591-7711, toll-free (Canada & U.S.) 1-800-268-9411
Visa, MC, Amex, enRoute, JCB

The Lodge at Kananaskis
The largest of the hotels at Kananaskis has 253 rooms, including some with two double beds, and other suites with fireplaces, lofts and whirlpools. It's swanky with facilities that include an indoor pool, health club, shops and boutiques and heated underground parking. Rates $76–$120.
Tel (403) 591-7711, toll-free (Canada & U.S.) 1-800-268-9411
Visa, MC, Amex, Diners, enRoute, JCB

Kananaskis Inn
The Inn has 90 rooms and suites, many with kitchens, which makes it a good bet for families; 32 of the rooms also have sleeping lofts. There's also an indoor pool. Rates $65–$110.
Tel (403) 591-7500
Visa, MC, Amex, Diners, enRoute, Discover

Inexpensive
Nearby Canmore (30 minutes away on Trans-Canada Hwy 1 towards Banff) is your best bet for inexpensive accommodations. There's a good supply of motels and hotels, and if you base yourself there you can easily scoot up to Banff if the chinook plays havoc with the snow at Nakiska.

Canmore Hotel
A fun place with sensible rooms, a dining room and live entertainment six nights a week. Rates $30–$45.
738 8th St. Tel (403) 678-5181
Visa, MC, Amex, T/CK

Best Run for Vertical
Eagle Tail–Bob Tail

Best Overall Run
Maverick–Mighty Peace

Best Restaurant
L'Escapade

Best Nightclub/Bar
Big Horn Lounge

Best Accommodation
Lodge at Kananaskis
Hugh Hancock, Nakiska

Kananaskis Taxi 591-7667

Timberline Towing 678-4249

Canmore Medical Centre
678-5536

Haus Alpenrose Lodge

Specializing in bed & breakfast, this all-purpose lodge has individual rooms, family-size suites and dormitories. Also has a central kitchen and a sauna. Rates $20–$75.

629 9th St. Tel (403) 678-4134

Visa, MC, T/CK

WHERE TO EAT

You won't go hungry in Kananaskis Village, though your choice is limited to the restaurants in the three major hotels. If you're looking for a little more variety, Canmore is about 30 minutes away along Trans-Canada Hwy 1.

Expensive

L'Escapade

L'Escapade features haute-French service, continental cuisine and European prices. Some of the edge is taken off the cost by the live harp or piano music, but it's definitely not the place to take the brood for a family meal. Reservations recommended.

In the Hotel Kananaskis. Tel 591-7711

Visa, MC, Amex, enRoute, JCB

The Peaks Dining Room

Not quite as pricey as L'Escapade, but still more suited to couples than to families. Specializes in Alberta beef, and has a good selection of other dishes. The Sunday brunch is particularly popular. Reservations recommended.

In the Lodge at Kananaskis. Tel 591-7711

Visa, MC, Amex, Diners, enRoute, Discover, JCB

MODERATE

Rockies Supper Club

A good spot for light dining, including pizza and pasta. Also features entertainment.

In the Lodge at Kananaskis. Tel 591-7711

Visa, MC, Amex, Diners, enRoute, Discover, JCB

Samurai Bar

For the raw fish crowd, the Samurai offers excellent sushi and sashimi, along with other traditional Japanese dishes such as tempura and shabu shabu.

In the Lodge at Kananaskis. Tel 591-7711

Visa, MC, Amex, Diners, enRoute, Discover, JCB

NIGHTLIFE

The entertainment in Kananaskis is centered around the three hotels and their assorted watering holes.

Loud and Lively

Big Horn Lounge

A little more low-key and less pub-like than Woodies. The Big Horn has its own brand of entertainment, but not the high-energy level of the pub.

In the Lodge at Kananaskis. Tel 591-7711

Woodies Pub

Live music, a young crowd, and the only place in the village if you're looking for some rock and roll to quaff your beer with. Also has a good choice of finger food and burgers.

In the Kananaskis Inn. Tel 591-7500

Mellow

Fireside Lobby Bar

Just about as low-key as you can get, the lobby bar is for those with not much on their mind but a quiet drink and some contemplative conversation before toddling off to bed.

In the Hotel Kananaskis. Tel 591-7711

DIVERSIONS

Canmore Nordic Centre

Of all the facilities created for the 1988 Winter Olympics, none gained the rave reviews that the Canmore Nordic Centre did. It has a superb network of track-set trails for both the traditional stride and gliders and the more aggressive skating set, with snowmaking guns to help out when nature doesn't cooperate. There are more than 62 mi (100 km) of trails, plus a superb day lodge area and numerous waxing huts along the network.

Imagine stepping out into a white void, ducking low to avoid the spinning blades of the chopper as it rises behind you, leaving you in the company of your twelve companions, crouched around a pile of skis in the midst of the pristine emptiness of a mountaintop. The clatter of the twentieth century veers away into the sky, and the silence of the white peaks envelops you.

The four-foot-deep dry, fluffy snow, untracked, beckons as you click into your skis. A guide leads off down the steep whiteness, you push off down the slope, the snow seethes up around your ankles, then your knees, slowing you until the pitch steepens, when you gather speed. The only sounds in the clear white wilderness are the swoosh of skis and the yelps of enraptured skiers. Welcome to heli-skiing.

There's no place on earth that has heli-skiing like Canada. Not the U.S. Rockies, not the Alps of Europe, not the glaciers of New Zealand. Nothing that even comes close to the pure adrenaline-pumping joy of skiing the Monashees, the Purcells, the Caribous and the Bugaboos. Sandwiched between the Rockies, which keep the cold air in the east, and the Coast Range, which wrings the moisture out of the snow to the west, there are more than 20,000 sq mi (52 500 km²) of mountains that give the very best ski experience that money can buy.

Stands of handsome spruce and fir form nature's own slalom course. They shield you from the wind and trap the snow in amounts so abundant that the wells are 10 ft (3 m) or deeper. This is where the very good skiers run—at full tilt, with controlled abandon.

So who are the skiers who ride the great white waves of ecstasy? Remarkably 80 percent of all the visitors to Canada's heli-skiing operators are from overseas—from the United States, Germany, France, Japan and other places far from the mountains of British Columbia. They come because they know there is nothing better. But very few Canadians take advantage of the best heli-skiing in the world even though it's in their own backyard. This is an anomaly that has heli-operators scratching their heads.

WHO CAN GO?

Anybody can go heli-skiing, so long as they are prepared to pay and are reasonably good, strong skiers. The most popular misconception is that you have to be a retired racer, or some other form of expert. But most heli-operators will tell you that being in good physical shape is more important than skiing skill. Groups are always divided by ability, and while some places may be so steep you'll weep, the limitless variety of terrain and snow conditions makes it possible to adjust the tempo and the challenge to suit varying abilities.

WHEN TO GO

Anytime between December and April. Although the best snow, the brightest weather and the highest price tags all happen in February and March, you can start or finish your season of sliding between those other months. Of course there are no guarantees where something as fickle as nature is concerned. As one deep snow junkie observed, "No matter what time of the year you choose, chopper skiing is the greatest, most expensive crap shoot you will ever play."

WHAT'S THE PRICE?

How does $3,000 a week sound? That's about average for an all-inclusive seven-day fun package that includes transportation from whichever western Canadian airport you arrive at, accommodation, meals, guides and approximately 100,000 ft (30 500 m) of vertical. That's the high-season price—February and March—but if you're in a penny-pinching mood take your chances in the off-season—December, January and April—and save $500 or $600.

HOW SAFE IS IT?

About once every two or three years, the heli-skier's worst fears are realized as an accident on some isolated mountain makes headlines. But it's only the bad news that makes news, and although the danger is inherent with skiing in the wilderness, the safety record of Canada's heli-skiing operators is exemplary.

Their safety procedures are stringent, from the detailed safety seminars that all heli-skiers must attend, to the daily computerized analyses of snow and weather conditions. But make no mistake, this is a risk sport. There are the avalanches, of course. And if you ski exactly where you are told by the guides—if you don't ski off alone, if you don't jump off a cliff—if you do precisely what you're told, then you'll come back in one piece. If you don't, then you could die. It's as a simple as that.

Canadian Mountain Holidays
Box 1660
Banff, Alberta
T0L 0M0
Tel (403) 762-4531
Has nine skiing locations in B.C.

Mike Wiegele Helicopter Skiing
Box 249
Banff, Alberta
T0L 0C0
Tel (403) 762-5548, toll-free (U.S.) 1-800-661-9170
Based in Blue River, B.C., three hours southwest of Marmot Basin

Great Canadian Heli-Skiing
Box 175
Golden, B.C.
V0A 1H0
Tel (604) 344-2326
60 mi (100 km) west of Banff, Alberta

Kootenay Helicopter Skiing
Box 717
Nakusp, B.C.
V0G 1R0
Tel (604) 265-3121, toll-free (B.C., Alberta & U.S.) 1-800-663-0100
90 minutes from Nelson, B.C.

Purcell Helicopter Skiing
Box 1530
Golden, B.C.
V0A 1H0
Tel (604) 344-5410
80 mi (130 km) west of Banff, Alberta

Selkirk Tangiers Helicopter Skiing
Box 1409
Golden, B.C.
V0A 1H0
Tel (604) 344-5016, toll-free (B.C., Alberta & U.S.) 1-800-663-7080
In Revelstoke, B.C.

Assiniboine Heli Tours
Box 2430
Canmore, Alberta
T0L 0M0
Tel (403) 678-5459
12 mi (20 km) east of Banff, Alberta

Chilco Lake Lodge
Box 6016
Williams Lake, B.C.
V2G 3W2
Tel (604) 481-1121
In the Coast Mountains, 230 mi (370 km) northeast of Vancouver

Island Lake Mountain Tours
Cedar Valley Rd
Fernie, B.C.
V0B 1M1
Tel (604) 423-3700
6 mi (10 km) from Fernie Snow Valley

FOR A HELI-EXPERIENCE OF A SHORTER KIND

If the price for a week of bliss has you shaking, or you're just not sure of your ability to handle the steep and the deep, then a day or half-day trip might be just the get-acquainted ticket. The following operators all have affordable introductory packages.

R.K. Heli-Ski Panorama
Box 695
Invermere, B.C.
V0A 1K0
Tel (604) 342-3889
At Panorama Ski Resort

Whistler Heli-Skiing
Box 368
Whistler, B.C.
V0N 1B0
Tel (604) 932-4105
At Whistler Ski Resort

Tyax Heli-Skiing
Box 849
Whistler, B.C.
V0N 1B0
Tel (604) 932-7007
At Whistler Ski Resort

Mountain Heli-Sports
Box 460
Whistler, B.C.
V0N 1B0
Tel (604) 932-2070
At Whistler Ski Resort

THE CAT-SKIING ALTERNATIVE

If you want to minimize the risk and the cost yet still sample some of the most outrageous deep snow, Cat-skiing is an alternative. The Snow Cats take you to virtually the same places the helicopters do, but at a fraction of the cost and with no hindrance from the weather. If it's snowing, foggy or just plain socked in, the Cats can still growl and you can still ski.

For a ground-level heli-skiing experience, try any of the following.

Great Northern Snow-Cat Skiing
Box 220, Station G
Calgary, Alberta
T3A 2G2
Tel (403) 287-2267
50 mi (80 km) north of Revelstoke, B.C.

Island Lake Mountain Tours
Cedar Valley Rd
Fernie, B.C.
V0B 1M1
Tel (604) 423-3700
6 mi (10 km) from Fernie Snow Valley

Lemon Creek Snowcat Skiing
Box 68
Slocan, B.C.
V0G 2C0
Tel (604) 355-2403
In the Slocan valley, 50 mi (80 km) north of Red Mountain

Selkirk Wilderness Skiing
1 Meadow Creek Rd
Meadow Creek, B.C.
V0G 1N0
Tel (604) 366-4424
80 mi (130 km) north of Nelson, B.C.

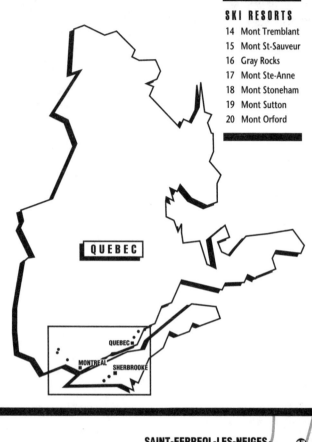

SKI RESORTS

14 Mont Tremblant
15 Mont St-Sauveur
16 Gray Rocks
17 Mont Ste-Anne
18 Mont Stoneham
19 Mont Sutton
20 Mont Orford

QUEBEC

QUEBEC

MONTREAL

SHERBROOKE

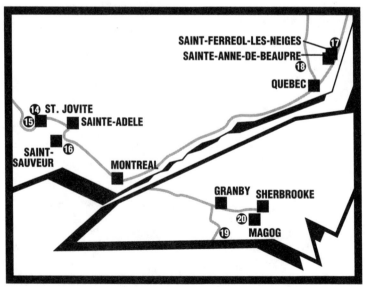

SAINT-FERREOL-LES-NEIGES
SAINTE-ANNE-DE-BEAUPRE

QUEBEC

ST. JOVITE
SAINTE-ADELE

SAINT-
SAUVEUR

MONTREAL

GRANBY SHERBROOKE

MAGOG

QUEBEC

The towering peaks of western Canada notwithstanding, there's no part of Canada that evokes images of winter sports, particularly skiing, than the province of Quebec. Starting on the western edge of the Canadian Shield and running east through the St Lawrence Lowlands and the rolling farmland of the Eastern Townships, then north of Quebec City up to the Gaspésie region, the province is a winter playground with more than a hundred alpine ski resorts and almost twice as many cross-country ski centers.

Most of the resorts lie within a narrow band 95 mi (150 km) north and south of the St Lawrence River. South of Montreal, amidst the pastoral farmlands of the Eastern Townships, is a collection of isolated peaks that are the remnants of the mighty Appalachian range, and north of Montreal the Laurentians, some of the oldest mountains on earth, cut east toward Quebec City. In these regions are the highest peaks and the best ski resorts in eastern Canada.

THE LAURENTIANS

HOW TO GET THERE

By Plane: The Laurentians are about 75 mi (120 km) north of Montreal. Dorval International Airport at Montreal is served by major airlines, with connections from major North American centers. Mirabel International Airport is about 25 mi (40 km) closer to the Laurentians, and handles international flights.

By Car: From Montreal the Laurentian Autoroute 15 runs north (with connections from all of Montreal's main expressways) to Ste-Agathe-des-Monts, where it connects with Hwy 117 north to St-Jovite.

By Bus: From the Montreal Voyageur Terminal (505 Maisonneuve ouest), Voyageur Bus Lines runs regularly scheduled trips to St-Jovite with stops in St-Sauveur and Ste-Agathe. Tel (514) 842-2281 (Montreal).

By Train: Via Rail has regular service to Montreal from across Canada. Amtrak runs regularly to Montreal, with connections from most U.S. centers.

The Laurentians, some of the oldest mountains in the world, form a rugged extension of the Appalachian mountain range and are home to the largest cluster of ski resorts in the country. From tiny Mont Habitant to mighty Mont Tremblant, they come in all shapes and sizes, with more than 20 resorts strung out along the Laurentian Autoroute from St-Jérôme to St-Jovite.

Most are small, local day-ski areas, but they all share this region's tradition of skiing, which dates back to the 1920s, when Montrealers began flocking north to experience a sport introduced by Norwegian expatriate Herman "Jackrabbit" Johannsen, who blazed the first cross-country trails and paved the way for what is now the region's largest industry. Parts of those early trails still exist throughout the valleys, meadows and forests of the area, and today there are 745 mi (1200 km) of marked and groomed trails across the entire region.

It was in the 1930s that signs of alpine skiing began to emerge. The first mechanical lift in North America was built, followed by the Laurentians' first T-bar in 1934 and the first chairlift in Canada in 1938. Soon came the famous ski trains, depositing fur-clad visitors along the way, where they were picked up by horse-drawn sleighs to be taken to the lodges, cabins and chalets that were making the Laurentians the Sun Valley of Canada.

Much of that style and elegance is gone now, but there's no mistaking that this is still ski country. There are two distinct areas, the lower (or middle) Laurentians, with St-Sauveur as its hub, and the upper Laurentians, with St-Jovite as the main center. St-Sauveur, with its bustling ski resort of the same name, is chic, a fur-and-high-fashion kind of town, filled on weekends with trendy Montrealers and the site of more than 50 restaurants, bars, bistros and nightclubs. St-Jovite is more staid, with more blue collar than blue fox. Still, it does have its appeal, with its lamp-lit streets, a decent number of restaurants and bars, and just down the road, two of the Laurentians' skiing giants, Mont Tremblant and Gray Rocks.

MONT TREMBLANT

3005 chemin Principale
Mont Tremblant, Quebec
J0T 1Z0
Tel (819) 425-8711;
toll-free (U.S. & Canada)
1-800-461-8711

No resort epitomized the grandeur and style of the *belle époque* of Laurentian skiing better than Mont Tremblant. When skiing was just catching on elsewhere in North America, it was already a tradition there. During its heyday in the 1950s and early 60s it was easily the rival of any resort in North America, with its wild terrain and vast collection of runs, its immense wood and stone lodge, surrounded by clusters of cottages, and its demand that gentlemen wear ties in the dining room.

Neckwear is no longer required in the dining room, but almost everything else from that period remains intact, and while resorts across the country have embarked upon hyperactive modernization sprees, this magnificent and storied mountain resort has managed to maintain its ambience, its flavor, its French flair and its timeless charm. Other resorts dream of having what Tremblant has.

And now in the 1990s it appears poised to write another chapter in its long history, and to do so with the money and the know-how its new owner, Intrawest (the builders and operators of Blackcomb Mountain), can provide. Long-range plans include a retro-fit of the base lodge area and the construction of expanded resort facilities on the south and north sides.

The mountain is still as wild and beautiful as it ever was, even with the addition of high-speed quad chairs, major-league snowmaking and the widening

Base Elevation:
870 ft (265 m)

Summit Elevation:
3,001 ft (915 m)

Vertical Drop:
2,131 ft (650 m)

Skiable Terrain:
296 acres (118 ha)

Number of Trails: 35

Longest Run: 3.4 mi (5.4 km)

Lifts & Capacity: 3 quads,
2 triples, 3 doubles, 2 T-bars;
15,600 skiers per hour

Daily Lift Ticket: $37
Weekly: $165 (5 days)

Annual Snowfall:
144 in (365 cm)

No. Days Skiing 91–92: 146

Snowmaking: 67%

Terrain Mix:
N 20%, I 46%, E 34%

Snow Phone: 1-800-461-8711

of its once narrow and challenging trails. The base village is in need of a facelift (something more than the recent addition of flimsy condo-style buildings), and many of the cabins and chalets are either as drafty as a bad tent or as unbearably hot as a coal-burning stove. But few resorts evoke the feeling that Tremblant does. A towering peak with skiing on both its south and north sides, the highest vertical in eastern Canada and 35 runs served by nine lifts, Tremblant is still the quintessential Quebec ski experience.

THE SKIING

Mont Tremblant is a Quebec classic and in many ways a throwback to the days when trails were narrow, steep and for the most part ungroomed. Only a few of the original runs are still the same as they were back in the 1940s and 50s; most have been widened and flattened for the more pampered skiers of the 80s.

Still, much of the rugged allure remains. Tremblant is a spectacular spire of a mountain that dwarfs all other peaks in the region, and from the summit under a strikingly blue Laurentian sky there's no vista anywhere in eastern Canada that compares.

The 2,131-ft (650-m) vertical is the highest in Quebec, and the 35 trails down the north and south sides are a good mixture of the long, the steep and the mogul-studded. With high-speed quads now running directly up to the summit, you can get the full measure of this mountain with top to bottom runs without the inconvenience of mid-mountain changes. Because some of the steeper pitches date back to a time when there was less regard for the sensitivities of aging yuppies, some such as Duncan and Devil's River provide an extra measure of excitement with their unpredictability.

Elsewhere on the mountain are some of the easiest-cruising novice runs anywhere—Nansen and Beauvallon both snake temptingly down and around the mountain—in direct contrast to the knee-shattering, bungalow-size bumps that predominate on Expo. And that's maybe the best aspect of skiing Mont Tremblant—the endless variety of pitch, length and trail conditions. Just as much variety is found in the weather; few places are as cold as Mont Tremblant. Yet few places are as stunningly beautiful when the sun is shining and the sky is a blue that is unmatched anywhere in the country.

HOW TO SKI MONT TREMBLANT

Novices

On the south side head for Nansen, one of the nicest novice cruising runs anywhere. On the north side try Sissy Schuss and Fuddle Duddle; both are long and well groomed.

Intermediates

Take a warm-up run on Beauchemin on the north side; it runs the full length of the mountain, providing a mixture of good steep—but wide—pitches, some interesting turns and drop-offs and plenty of room for fast giant slalom turns. Tuck the lower portion to make it to the north-side base area. Head back up to the top and try Upper and Lower Duncan or Devil's River. On the south side try McCullough for some good steep skiing, or Ryan's for more of the same.

Experts

When there's good snow coverage, you have to ski Expo, a mean mogul-studded brute on the north side. Ski the left side for the biggest bumps and some challenging drop-offs. On the south side the Flying Mile is a beautiful full-bore cruiser, with excellent pitch and room to let your skis run. Also try Lowell Thomas and Devil's River for variety.

WHERE TO STAY

All accommodation in the Mont Tremblant area can be booked through Central Reservations at (514) 436-8532, or through Mont Tremblant Reservations at 1-800-567-6760 (toll-free Canada & U.S.), a privately operated reservation service that also rents private chalets, cabins and condos.

Expensive

Club Tremblant
One of the nicest hotel and condo complexes at Tremblant, the Club is on the shores of Lac Tremblant overlooking the mountain. There's a combination of hotel rooms in the main hotel, and a collection of modern condo units with one and two bedrooms. The condo units have kitchen, living room and fireplace. Rates $110–$142 per person including two meals and lift tickets.
Ave Cuttles. Tel (819) 425-2731, toll-free (Canada) 1-800-567-8341, toll-free (U.S.) 1-800-363-2413
Visa, MC, Amex, enRoute

Mont Tremblant Resort
I like staying at the lodge, not so much for its modern amenities as for its convenience and rustic ambience. It does have its drawbacks: the rooms in the main lodge and the adjacent buildings are small, spartan in furnishings and cursed with notoriously thin walls. Better are the cabins and chalets—some with three bedrooms and fireplaces—that are scattered about the base village area. They are not fancy, but setting and proximity to the lifts make up for that. Rates $125–$340 per person for 2 nights.
Tel (819) 425-8711, toll-free (Canada & U.S.) 1-800-461-8711
Visa, MC, Amex

Moderate

Auberge La Porte Rouge
If you favor the smaller country inn ambience, this is a good choice. The rooms are fairly standard, but the location in the center of Mont Tremblant Village is great. Several chalets are available. Rates $375–$415 per person per week including meals and lift tickets.
Tel (819) 425-3505
Visa, MC

Chalet des Chutes
A cute spot just a mile (1.5 km) from the mountain, the hotel-style rooms are basic yet comfortable, and there's a nice feel to the place even if it isn't fancy. A TV room is the extent of the amenities. Also has some small one- and two-bedroom chalets. Rates $85–$110 including meals and lift tickets.
2749 chemin Principale, Mont Tremblant. Tel (819) 425-2738

Château Beauvallon

A rustic and intimate ski lodge operated by its owners and situated on about 4 acres (1.5 ha) of wooded grounds about a mile (1.5 km) from the mountain. I like this place for its French-Canadian ambience and hospitality. Basic yet cozy and comfortable rooms. Rates $370–$415 per person for 6 nights, including meals and lift tickets.

Montée Ryan. Tel (819) 425-7275

Amex, CK

Le Pinoteau Village

A collection of 50 condo units set high on a hill about a mile (1.5 km) from the mountain, Pinoteaus is a Mont Tremblant classic. The units are large and fully equipped with kitchen, fireplace, TV and dishwasher. There's a whirlpool and health club along with laundry facilities. Rates $110–$180 (1-bedroom), $157–$241 (2-bedroom).

Pinoteau Village St. Tel (819) 425-2795, toll-free (Canada) 1-800-667-2200

Visa, MC

Villa Bellevue

This family-run hotel about 3 mi (5 km) from the mountain is another favorite of mine, and it's especially suited to family groups. Rooms range from standard to deluxe with fireplaces. It also has a great sports center with swimming pool, sauna, steam bath and exercise room. Rates $110–$130 including two meals and lift tickets.

845 chemin Principale, Lac Ouimet. Tel (819) 425-2734, toll-free 1-800-567-6763

Visa, MC, Amex, enRoute

Inexpensive

Auberge Escapade

A cozy little family-run inn that looks a bit like a renovated barn. It's a little bit away from the action—about 2 mi (3 km) from the slopes—but it has a countryside ambience that's hard to beat. Rooms are basic and comfortable. Ski packages start at $248 per person for 5 nights, including lift tickets and two meals a day.

2213 chemin Principale, Mont Tremblant. Tel (819) 425-7311

Visa, MC

Hôtel Mont Tremblant
A truly funky hotel in the middle of the village of Mont Tremblant. Its 30 rooms are small and basic, and you may find the noise from the downstairs bar a little overwhelming, but overall a good deal and a good location. Rates $37–$48.
1900 rue Principale, Mont Tremblant. Tel (819) 425-3232
Visa, MC, Amex

WHERE TO EAT
All of the major hotels have their own dining rooms, ranging from the superb to the average. If you book a ski week package, you take what you get. For those who choose to pick their own spots, here's what I recommend.

Expensive
Club Tremblant
This has to be one of the best dining rooms in the area. Mostly a continental menu, but lots of local specialties, divine sauces and exquisite desserts. Also a great view from the dining room. If you're on a ski week package at Club Tremblant, you probably won't want to eat anywhere else. For those residing elsewhere, this is one hotel dining room worth checking out. Reservations recommended.
In the Club Tremblant, ave Cuttles. Tel 425-2731
Visa, MC, Amex, enRoute

La Saucière
A distinctively French menu that is as good as any in the area and always features daily specials. The service is excellent, and the setting elegant. Reservations recommended.
1991 chemin Principale, Mont Tremblant. Tel 425-7575
Visa, MC

Moderate
Antipastos
A real favorite of mine, it's recently moved to a renovated train station at the south end of St-Jovite. Great pasta, incredible designer pizza baked in brick ovens and various other Italian specialties. Great atmosphere, and always busy.
855 Ouimet, St-Jovite. Tel 425-7580
Visa, MC

Best Run for Vertical
Kandahar

Best Overall Run
Ryan/Lower Ryan

Best Restaurant
La Saucière

Best Nightclub/Bar
Au Coin

Best Accommodation
Club Tremblant
  Neil Vinet, Mont Tremblant

**MONT TREMBLANT—
USEFUL TELEPHONE
NUMBERS**
(area code 819)

Tourism Association
425-3300

Ambulance 425-2726

Medical Centre—St-Jovite
425-2728

Voyageur Bus Line (St-Jovite)
425-3115

L'Abbé du Nord

A good spot for more traditional North American fare, but steaks and ribs are the real specialty. Also has a great salad bar for the light-biters.
In Mont Tremblant Village. Tel 425-8394
No cards

La Bagatelle

Good French cuisine with daily specials and a nicely varied menu. Country-style cooking with lots of fresh ingredients.
852 Ouimet, St-Jovite. Tel 425-5323
Visa, MC

O Wok

This is St-Jovite's official Chinese restaurant, and through all its many name changes it remains *the* spot for a typical Chinese chow-down.
878 Ouimet, St-Jovite. Tel 425-8442
Visa, MC, Amex

Inexpensive

Restaurant Lorraine

An excellent family restaurant that has a great selection of standard items such as chicken, pizza, smoked meats and burgers. Hearty, cheap and fast.
2000 chemin Principale, Mont Tremblant. Tel 425-5566

NIGHTLIFE

Loud and Lively

Au Coin

A popular spot with locals, it's a loud and pounding place spread over several rooms and vestibules. Great music, lots of games and a young crowd that dances up a storm far into the night.
In the Hôtel Mont Tremblant, 1900 rue Principale, Mont Tremblant. Tel 425-3232

Express Bar
The Express doesn't cook until after dinner, but then it's disco and dance music, flashing lights and a flashy, exuberant crowd.
Downstairs in the Mont Tremblant Resort. Tel 425-8711

Musicale Bar
An upbeat and dance-oriented atmosphere. Usually has live entertainment playing a range of music that suits the slightly older crowd.
In the Villa Bellevue, 845 chemin Principale, Lac Ouimet. Tel 425-2734

Octagon
The *only* place to head after skiing at Mont Tremblant. At the bottom of the south side, at the end of the day lodge, the Octagon is informal, rough-hewn and fills up fast with a crowd that drinks Laurentide beer and laughs up a storm. There's loud music, multiple TVs, impromptu dancing, and on warm sunny days the crowd spills onto the sundeck, where late arrivals can conveniently snag a brew without stepping out of their skis.

Thirsty Eagle Bar (see Gray Rocks)

Mellow
Bistro Bar
This is a quietly elegant spot for low-key cocktails and conversation. Usually has live entertainment with classical duos or trios.
In the Mont Tremblant Resort, Lac Tremblant. Tel 425-8711

Club Tremblant Piano Bar
A great place to enjoy a quieter moment, and a superb view out over Lac Tremblant. Elegant, sophisticated and stylish. There's occasionally live entertainment of the cocktail variety, and a pleasant cozy ambience that's perfect for couples.
In the Club Tremblant, ave Cuttles. Tel 425-2731

GRAY ROCKS

Box 1000
St-Jovite, Quebec
J0T 2H0
Tel (819) 425-2771

HOW TO GET THERE

By Car: Gray Rocks is 3 mi
(5 km) from the town of St-
Jovite. From Montreal, take
the Laurentian Autoroute
north; 19 mi (30 km) after
the merge with Hwy 117,
take the first exit for St-
Jovite. At the first traffic light
turn right on Hwy 327 north
to the resort.

By Bus: Voyageur Bus Lines
runs regularly scheduled
service from Montreal to St.
Jovite. Gray Rocks runs a
connecting free shuttle
service from the town to the
resort.

It's hard to describe exactly what makes Gray Rocks one of the most popular resorts in Canada. It's overshadowed in size by Mont Tremblant, just 3 mi (5 km) down the road, and nearby St-Sauveur has more cachet and appeal for the Montreal crowd. Yet year after year the sprawling resort founded by the Wheeler family more than 60 years ago continues its remarkable record of drawing skiers from all over North America.

Not that Gray Rocks is without its virtues. It's the country's most prolific producer of artificial snow— about 15 ft (4.5 m) annually—which gives it a ski season that lasts from November to May. It's similarly renowned for its ski school program, which I think is one of the best on the continent. And it's the originator of the ski week concept, which combines skiing, instruction, accommodation, meals and Club Med–like good times in one well-organized package.

Still, it is remarkable that an unremarkable mogul of a mountain with barely 600 ft (180 m) of vertical could have carved such a niche for itself in the highly competitive Canadian ski market.

Tucked on the shores of picturesque Lac Ouimet, it is a large, sprawling resort spread over 2,000 acres (800 ha), with the rambling Gray Rocks Inn as its centerpiece. The original inn was built back in 1906 and remains the hub of the much expanded resort facilities. Inside there are over 200 rooms of varying sizes. Recent additions include a health spa and fitness center, but the traditional mainstays of the inn—the Thirsty Eagle Bar, the cavernous dining room and the smaller fireside lounges—are the essence of Gray Rocks. New additions to the property include a smaller inn plus a collection of condominium units, but the look of the place has remained essentially

GRAY ROCKS— STATISTICALLY SPEAKING

Base Elevation:
830 ft (253 m)

Summit Elevation:
1,440 ft (440 m)

Vertical Drop: 620 ft (190 m)

Skiable Terrain:
52 acres (21 ha)

Number of Trails: 20

Longest Run:
1,400 ft (427 m)

Lifts & Capacity: 1 quad,
3 doubles; 5,600 skiers per hour

Daily Lift Ticket: $23;
multi-day discounts

Annual Snowfall:
110 in (280 cm)

No. Days Skiing 91–92: 160

Snowmaking: 85%

Terrain Mix:
N 33%, I 29%, E 38%

Snow Phone: 1-800-567-6767

unchanged for more than half a century.

The skiing is on adjacent Sugar Mountain, a pretty but unimposing knob of land on the far side of Hwy 327 as it winds its way up from St-Jovite to Mont Tremblant. It's there that the reputation of Gray Rocks was built, with the widely acclaimed Snow Eagles ski instructors imparting their knowledge and sharing their packaged bonhomie with skiers from as far away as Texas. (Americans have always been the most consistent visitors to the resort, and still make up almost 80 percent of its ski week participants.)

The ski week is what Gray Rocks is all about, and it remains one of the best values in Canadian alpine skiing.

THE SKIING

Sugar Mountain packs a lot of variety into its 20 runs and 620 ft (190 m) of vertical, and the one thing you can always be sure of is the consistency of the snow. Snowmaking is virtually a round-the-clock affair from November to March, and the result is a dependable, meticulously groomed collection of runs that seldom if ever show a bare spot or an icy section. One quad and three double chairlifts cover the mountain, so even if the runs don't go forever (which they don't) you can fit a lot of skiing into a single day.

Snowmaking and ski instruction are what stand out at Gray Rocks, and they make a tidy little package that more than compensates for the smallish size of the mountain. As one somewhat jaded visitor remarked after a week in the clutches of the famous Snow Eagles ski school, "I've skied all over the world from Spain to Aspen, and I never learned as much about technique as I did in the past five days."

Best Run for Vertical
Réal Charette

Best Overall Run
Bonaventure

Best Restaurant
Antipastos

Best Nightclub/Bar
Thirsty Eagle Bar

Best Accommodation
Village des Soleils
Paul King, Gray Rocks

GRAY ROCKS (ST-JOVITE)—
USEFUL TELEPHONE
NUMBERS
(area code 819)

Medical Centre 425-2728

Voyageur Bus Lines 425-3115

HOW TO SKI GRAY ROCKS

Novices

Try Vagabond on the west side for a warm-up run, then take a long run on La Portage. Chipmunk is another long, wide run from the top of the double chair on the north side.

Intermediates

Take the double chair up the east side and try a long cruise of Lucille Wheeler. Go back up and turn right to Niagara, taking it all the way to the bottom. Next take the chair up the west side and try a fast run on Bonaventure. For some bumps try either Réal Charette or Les Bouleaux.

Experts

Head up the north-side chair and take a crack at the steep and bumpy Gadner or the even steeper and narrower Apollo. Next head for the west side and have some fun on the short but bumpy runs through the trees on either Bon Voyage or Devil's Dip. To let the skis run a little, try Rapido off the same lift.

WHERE TO STAY

Most visitors to Gray Rocks partake of the all-inclusive ski week package, since it affords the most convenience and the best price. If you prefer to be away from the Club Med atmosphere, you can stay in the Mont Tremblant/St-Jovite area, just a 10-minute drive from Gray Rocks.

At Gray Rocks, both the main inn and the newer, smaller Château are priced to include breakfast and dinner, along with the skiing and instruction package.

All accommodation at the resort can be booked through the toll-free (Canada & U.S.) Central Reservations number, 1-800-567-6767.

Moderate

Gray Rocks Inn

This rambling 280-room hotel has mostly basic rooms, along with some upgraded and renovated rooms featuring fireplaces and balconies. There are three deluxe suites. Beware, the basic rooms are just that. If you're looking for a little more space, renovated rooms and a quieter location in the complex, pick either the superior or deluxe package. Rates from $620 per person for 6 nights with meals, up to $920 for one of the suites.

Le Château

A smaller, more modern inn with 24 rooms, about a five-minute walk from the slopes. Rooms can accommodate up to three guests. Rates $79–$142 per person.

Village des Soleils

I particularly like these luxury condo units just five minutes from the slopes. It's the only accommodation that does not come with the mandatory meal plan. The units come in one, two or three bedrooms and include all the luxury trimmings with fully equipped kitchens. Rates $350–$490 per person for 6 nights without meals; $690–$820 with meals.

A Word about Gray Rocks Packages

While there's no doubt that the all-inclusive package at Gray Rocks is a great deal, and there's no better way to upgrade your skiing, it is not necessarily for those who like their freedom and choice. Some may find the morning-to-night organization and constant bonhomie of group participation isn't their style. Some people may also prefer to explore the many fine restaurants in the area rather than be locked into a hotel meal package.

But keep in mind that it is possible to avail yourself of a technique tune-up without sacrificing your freedom.

TRIP TO TREMBLANT

As you're scooting down the slopes of Sugar Peak, the ever-so-tempting summit of larger Mont Tremblant is off in the distance. With its higher elevation and longer runs, it's a shame not to pay a visit. Although the basic all-inclusive package does provide for days at the big mountain, intermediate and advanced skiers should consider the Tremblant add-on package, which takes you to that resort every day in the company of the venerable Gray Rocks Snow Eagle Ski School.

NIGHTLIFE

Life after ski is part of the all-inclusive Gray Rocks ski week package, and the Thirsty Eagle Bar in the main inn is focused on fun. Happy hour—and I do mean happy—starts immediately after skiing, and the pace is non-stop frenetic until the first dinner call. After the second dinner sitting, the pace picks up again, with live entertainment, pep talks from the Snow Eagles and dancing. It's well orchestrated, well placed within stumbling distance of all the on-site accommodation and as much a part of the ski week experience as the action on the slopes.

For variations in nightlife, see Mont Tremblant.

LOWER LAURENTIANS

The lower or middle Laurentians, about 30 mi (50 km) south of the Mont Tremblant/St-Jovite area, has the largest concentration of small ski areas anywhere in the country. Most are lit for night skiing, giving the area the largest number of lighted trails in Canada, and most are found within a few minutes of the Autoroute. One of these smaller regional centers deserves to be included among the best resorts in the country, and that is Mont St-Sauveur.

MONT ST-SAUVEUR

Box 910
St-Sauveur-des-Monts,
Quebec
J0R 1R0
Tel (514) 227-4671

HOW TO GET THERE
By Car: St-Sauveur is about 37 mi (60 km) north of Montreal via the Laurentian Autoroute. Take Exit 60 and follow the signs for St-Sauveur.

By Bus: Voyageur Bus Lines runs regular trips to St-Sauveur from Montreal.

In the center of the bustling St-Sauveur valley, Mont St-Sauveur is as much about lifestyle as it is about skiing. The village is a busy mélange of winding streets filled with all manner of restaurants—the largest concentration of dining spots outside any major city—bars, bistros, shops, boutiques, galleries and gift shops. It's a place to stroll, to browse, to window shop and take in everything from the smell of freshly baked croissants in the early morn to the torrid nightlife and night skiing that carry on till the wee hours.

THE SKIING

By any standards, Mont St-Sauveur is not big. Its 26 trails stretched across a ridge that overlooks the town have a vertical of only 700 ft (213 m), but it compensates in other ways. The sophisticated snowmaking covers 90 percent of the skiable terrain, and the nine lifts, including four quad chairs, move the mob about efficiently. The layout is pretty straightforward, with the runs shooting straight down off the ridge (including the seven runs of adjacent Mont Avila, which is now part of the St-Sauveur complex).

You won't need a trail map here, unless it's to avoid some of the steeper black diamond runs, and a good steady intermediate skier will be able to try all

MONT ST-SAUVEUR— STATISTICALLY SPEAKING

Base Elevation:
656 ft (200 m)

Summit Elevation:
1,355 ft (413 m)

Vertical Drop: 700 ft (213 m)

Skiable Terrain:
142 acres (57 ha)

Number of Trails: 26

Longest Run: 0.9 mi (1.4 km)

Lifts & Capacity: 4 quads,
2 triples, 2 doubles,
1 surface; 14,100 skiers per
hour

Daily Lift Ticket: $30
Weekly: $125

Annual Snowfall:
110 in (250 cm)

No. Days Skiing 91–92: 125

Snowmaking: 90%

Terrain Mix:
N 20%, I 50%, E 30%

Snow Phone: 1-800-363-2426
(Canada)

trails in a single day. The easier beginner runs are at either end of the ridge, winding down in gentle undulating fashion. All the runs are boulevard smooth, thanks to relentless snow grooming, and the up-and-down action doesn't stop when the sun goes down because 90 percent of the trails are lit for night skiing.

And when you're tired out from skiing, the stylish base lodge—part restaurant, part activity center and part stage—is invariably filled with alternative entertainment. If balloons and sky divers don't fill the sky, live bands and outdoors barbecues offer a non-stop diversion. St-Sauveur is simply one of the best-run and most entertaining slices of ski life found anywhere in the country.

HOW TO SKI ST-SAUVEUR

Novices

Stick to the outer perimeter of the ridge, following the green trails that give you the longest and smoothest runs on the mountain.

Intermediates

The three runs on either side of the main lift are pure intermediate territory, with good steady pitch. Intermediates also won't find more than they can handle on the five black diamond runs on the Avila side of the ridge.

Experts

You can ski anywhere, but the six black diamond runs on the right side of the ridge give you the best mix of steepness and bumps.

Expensive

Hôtel Châteaumont
A five-minute drive from the slopes, and even less from all the village action, this hotel has 32 fairly luxurious rooms, some with a fireplace. Rates $85–$140.
50 rue Principale. Tel (514) 227-1821
Visa, MC, Amex, Diners, enRoute

Le Manoir St-Sauveur
This is a great resort hotel with all the trimmings including an indoor pool, health club, squash courts and sauna. There are 150 luxury rooms and suites, and the location in the middle of town means you are just steps from all the action. Rates $89–$109 per person.
246 chemin du Lac Millette. Tel (514) 227-1811, toll-free (U.S. & Canada) 1-800-361-0505
Visa, MC, Amex, Diners, enRoute

Village Mont St-Sauveur
A luxury condo complex that offers the only true slopeside accommodation. The 300 units range from one to three bedrooms and are fully equipped with everything from kitchen to fireplace. Rates $120–$180.
600 Avila St, Piedmont. Tel (514) 227-4671, toll-free (U.S. & Canada) 1-800-363-2426
Visa, MC, Amex

Moderate

Auberge Les Amériques
The rooms are fairly large but fairly basic, with none of the luxury trimmings. A convenient mid-town location, five minutes from the slopes. Rates $40–$65 per person.
101 rue Principale. Tel (514) 227-1831
Visa, MC, Amex, enRoute

Auberge St Denis

A combination of hotel-type rooms at the Auberge and a selection of luxury condos right in the heart of St-Sauveur. Rates $79–$109.

61 St Denis. Tel (514) 227-4766

Visa, MC, Amex, Diners

Inexpensive

Pension du Cap

For something a little different I recommend this bed & breakfast. About 10 minutes from the mountain, it has a dozen comfortable rooms and an overall good feeling about it. Rates $35–$45 per person.

270 chemin Constantineau. Tel (514) 227-3424

No cards

WHERE TO EAT

Expensive

Da Tulio's

A haute-cuisine restaurant, with the emphasis on Italian. Incredible veal dishes, fantastic homemade pasta, plus service and style to match. Reservations recommended.

389 rue Principale. Tel 227-4313

Visa, MC, Amex

Marie Philip

If price is no object and style is everything, the hottest upscale restaurant in town should be your choice. Marie Philip is small and features French cooking, nouvelle style. The breast of chicken with pear vinegar and wild rice is outstanding, the tournedos of salmon and the salmon tartare heavenly, and the casserole of scallops sublime. Presentation, service and image are superb here.

352 rue Principale. Tel 227-2171

Visa, MC, Amex, enRoute

Moderate

Best Run for Vertical
Hill 71

Best Overall Run
Hill 71

Best Restaurant
Moe's Deli and Bar

Best Nightclub/Bar
Bourbon Street

Best Accommodation
Village Mont St-Sauveur
  Gilles Auger,
  St-Sauveur-des-Monts

ST-SAUVEUR—USEFUL
TELEPHONE NUMBERS
(area code 514)

Ambulance 229-3525

Medical Centre—St-Jerome
432-9711

Chamber of Commerce
227-2564

Laurentians Tourism Bureau
436-8532

Voyageur Bus Lines 842-2281

Gibby's
Gibby's is a long-time favorite with the red-meat crowd. It also features an excellent rack of lamb, and the veal chops are particularly good. For dessert, try the gâteau St-Honoré.
414 rue Principale. Tel 227-2623
Visa, MC, Amex, Diners, enRoute, Discover

La Bohème
This intimate bistro/restaurant is a new favorite of mine. The menu is mainly French with some interesting daily specials. The wine list offers some products not widely available.
251 rue Principale. Tel 227-6644
No cards

Le Kindli
This Swiss-style restaurant has been a tradition in St-Sauveur for as long as I can remember. Its motif and decor is pure Swiss, and the fare includes such regional specialties as raclette and fondue. Try the Kindlie cordon bleu for a real treat.
22 Lafleur North. Tel 227-2229
Visa, MC, Amex, enRoute

Inexpensive
Giorgio's
If it's a pasta-fest you have in mind, Giorgio's will give you your fill at prices that are hard to believe. All the traditional dishes, plus some veal and chicken specialties.
At the junction of the Laurentian Autoroute and Hwy 15. Tel 227-3151
Visa, MC, Amex

Moe's Deli and Bar
If your appetite is bigger than the nearby mountains, head over to Moe's for oversize portions of traditional deli fare. The smoked meat is particularly good. Also has such staples as steaks and pizza. Beware if you order large servings—they may have to carry you out.
21 rue Delajare. Tel 227-8803
Visa, MC, Amex

NIGHTLIFE
Loud and Lively
Bentley's
Part restaurant and part bar, Bentley's is a bustling place that serves good finger food such as wings, potato skins and chicken fingers, and also serves up lots of evening revelry at its large stand-up bar. A fun place and an in place. Worth checking out.
235 rue Principale. Tel 227-1851

Bourbon Street
This place really rocks, with great music, dancing and lots of mingling. It's a major draw throughout the region, and even its isolated location doesn't detour the demonic crowd that gathers there.
2045 Hwy 117, between Piedmont and Ste-Adèle. Tel 229-2905

The Bulldozer Bar
Although I haven't had the pleasure of sampling the Bulldozer, I have it on absolute authority that this is the place to go for local color. And I do mean color. There's no entertainment, save the patrons, and the atmosphere is pure tavern, with the beer in those large quart bottles.
241 rue Principale. Tel 227-4996

The Commons Bar
For the younger, less well heeled crowd, the Commons is the perfect place to party until you're pooped. Live rock bands every weekend, and dancing to a different beat.
73 Lac Echo Rd, Morin Heights. Tel 226-2211

La Nuit Blanche
Definitely a late-night spot for those in a mood to party to live entertainment (occasionally). If it's not live, then it is loud, and the dancing is non-stop. A spot to be seen in.
762 rue Principale, Piedmont. Tel 227-5419

O'Toole's
One of the chain cut from the traditional roadhouse mold, this is a bit of a change for sophisticated St-Sauveur. Good music, lots of young people and tons of late-night action.
220 chemin du Lac Millette. Tel 227-3619

Mellow
Resto Polo
A good spot to sit back and savor the day. Usually has live entertainment in the form of a solo singer, and the atmosphere is cozy enough to allow romance to blossom. A good spot for that final nightcap.
307 rue Principale. Tel 227-2430

Les Vieilles Portes
A truly stylish enclave built by a prince (his origins and title obscure enough to be ignored) more than a hundred years ago, this large mansion features a massive hand-carved wooden bar, stone walls and original oil paintings. Lots of comfy couches and chairs, a crackling fireplace and subdued music.
185 rue Principale. Tel 227-2662

THE EASTERN TOWNSHIPS

HOW TO GET THERE
By Plane: Montreal is the gateway city for the Eastern Townships. Dorval and Mirabel international airports are served by major airlines, with connections from major centers.

By Car: From Montreal, cross the St Lawrence River on the Champlain Bridge, then follow the signs for the Eastern Townships Autoroute, Hwy 10 (also known as the Autoroute Cantons de l'Est).

The Eastern Townships (the Cantons de l'Est) are located directly south of Montreal, near the Vermont border. That in part accounts for the delightful mélange of English and French inhabitants, many of whose ancestors settled the land.

That mixed heritage has continued with a fraternal bilingualism that is rare in the province of Quebec. There are predominantly English-speaking communities such as Knowlton and Mansonville and clusters of French-speaking towns such as Bromont and Magog, and in between communities where the two languages are both used freely. History is alive in the region, with sleepy hamlets that haven't changed much since the 1800s, elegant Victorian mansions and sturdy covered wooden bridges. In addition to the collection of English and French names, you'll find vestiges of the original inhabitants, the Abenaki Indians, in the form of such tongue-twisting placenames as Memphrémagog, Massawippi and Coaticook.

At first glance the Townships don't look like ski country. Unlike the Laurentians to the north, where the terrain includes rock promontories and mountain ridges, the Townships are a varied mixture of rolling farmland and isolated mountain peaks separated by low valleys, sprawling across 4,940 sq mi (13 000 km^2). It wasn't until the early 1960s that the first ski resort was established here, but in the 30 years since, eight alpine and 20 cross-country centers have sprung up, ranging from small local areas to the two biggest and best alpine areas in the region, Mont Sutton and Mont Orford.

MONT SUTTON

Box 280
Sutton, Quebec
J0E 2K0
Tel (514) 538-2338

HOW TO GET THERE

By Car: Mont Sutton is a 90-minute drive from Montreal. Cross the St Lawrence River on the Champlain Bridge and follow signs for Hwy 10 (Autoroute Cantons de l'est). Take Exit 68 and follow Hwy 139 into Sutton.

By Bus: Voyageur Bus Lines operates a regular bus service from Montreal.

Mont Sutton lies about 2 mi (3 km) outside of the town of Sutton and has been a favorite of mine since the days when the fiercely independent family of owners eschewed the merits of snowmaking in favor of a more labor-intensive method they called snow farming: moving nature's bounty around the mountain with snowcats and bulldozers. The practice eventually did give way to more practical snowmaking technology, but the same family still owns and operates the resort.

The Boulangers are that family, and the patriarch, the late Réal, created Mont Sutton in the early 1960s with a zeal and a vision that today's ski entrepreneurs can only marvel at. Granted, he had some fine raw material to work with. Mont Sutton is the highest of the Township's mountains at 2,900 ft (884 m), and Réal knew every inch of it intimately. He studied the fall lines and followed them religiously when he cut the trails; he also built an extensive system of secondary trails so skiers could mix and match main-run sections. Most enduring of all was his love of trees, tall stands of maple, spruce and birch that he adamantly refused to cut down.

And therein lies his legacy: the Sous Bois, or glades, the major allure of the most varied and delightful 174 acres (70 ha) of ski terrain one could wish for. And everyone can savor the joy of skiing the trees, for every one of Sutton's nine lifts has at least one glade run, and to steam down them on a sunny day after a heavy snowfall when they are filigreed in a delicate white frosting is an unforgettable experience.

That attention to detail and to the needs of skiers is apparent in other aspects of Mont Sutton, from its spacious base lodge facilities, with ample room for the brown-bag set and simple wholesome, home-cooked fare in the restaurant, to the coziness of the

MONT SUTTON— STATISTICALLY SPEAKING

Base Elevation:
1,400 ft (427 m)

Summit Elevation:
2,900 ft (884 m)

Vertical Drop:
1,500 ft (457 m)

Skiable Terrain:
174 acres (70 ha)

Number of Trails: 53

Longest Run: 2 mi (3.2 km)

Lifts & Capacity: 3 quads,
6 double chairs; 11,800 skiers
per hour

Daily Lift Ticket: $37
Weekly: $141 (5 days)

Annual Snowfall:
192 in (488 cm)

No. Days Skiing 91–92: 158

Snowmaking:
104 acres (42 ha)

Terrain Mix:
N 30%, I 40%, E 30%

Snow Phone: 866-5156/7639

summit lodge, with its crackling fire, hearty pea soup served from steaming cauldrons and a view from the deck that even Réal never grew tired of seeing.

The resort has its other virtues, including the nearby town of Sutton, a delightful little collection of galleries, boutiques, ski shops, restaurants, bistros, inns and auberges. Just minutes down the road from the mountain, this charming community is almost an extension of the resort. Separate or together, they provide a special blend of the traditional and the progressive.

Visitors should pick up a copy of *La Tour*. It's the local paper, widely available, and filled with news of all the local action and activities.

THE SKIING

For those who measure the challenge of their ski experience by the vertical, there's a big surprise in store at Mont Sutton. Its modest 1,500 ft (457 m) of vertical conceals as wide a variety of skiing as it's possible to find at one resort. If you can ski every one of the 53 trails, along with all the variations that the layout encourages, you're better than most.

The Sous Bois, or glade runs, alone offer enough variety and options to keep you guessing and picking new routes for a day or more. Another thing you'll notice at Sutton is the narrowness of the trails, trails unaffected by the demands of today's highway cruisers. They groom at Sutton, on a rotating basis, but that doesn't mean a totally flat surface from one side of the trail to the other, and the stands of trees coddle and protect the snow in delicious and unpredictable mounds. To the Boulangers, snow and trees are the natural enhancers of the ski experience, and all levels of skiers will find new challenges in the philosophy. You may find yourself taking a slightly easier run than normal, but once you catch the rhythm of the runs, there's always excitement around the next corner.

The inter-linking of the 53 named trails is another Sutton trait that takes some getting used to, but again, once you get a feel for the mix-and-match layout, you'll add spice to your experience. In this regard, make sure you carry a trail map at Sutton. The terrain can become confusing, especially at the many intersections.

The layout runs from west to east, with the easier terrain on the western side, the intermediate territory in the middle, and the expert stuff on the east ridge. Actually novice skiers can find a way down from the top of any of the lifts, and a long, winding trail called Access gives you a bail-out to the base area from almost anywhere on the mountain.

HOW TO SKI MONT SUTTON

Novices
Head for Lift 2, to the right of the lodge as you look up the mountain. From there you can access other lifts, but I recommend the Alleghenys for your first test of the mountain. It runs from the top of Lift 1V all the way down to the bottom of Lift 1.

Intermediates
Take the detachable quad chair on the left side of the lodge and try a couple of warm-up runs on Mohawk or Caprice, or get right into the glades on Sous Bois 11. To get over to the eastern side, take Youppe Youppe to the base of Lift 4.

Experts
Take the quad to the top, then ski down Sous Bois Youp to the bottom of Lift 4, then up to the top of the mountain for the glade experience. The variety is great on this side, and you may want to combine three trails: Sous Bois V, Alpine and Escapade; they are steep, wide and packed with trees.

TRY BEFORE YOU BUY
Sutton has a unique ticketing arrangement that allows you to sample the mountain before you commit to a full day on the slopes. It's skiing by the hour: the first costs $12, each successive hour $6. You pay in advance and are refunded for any unskied time. It's especially great for that last day when you have time only for a couple of hours on the slopes and don't want to buy a full-day lift ticket.

WHERE TO STAY

Most accommodations in the Sutton area, from brand-new condo units to the many small inns, offer the full ski week package, which includes meals and lift tickets, and in some cases the pro-rated cost of the room can work out to be less than $20 a night.

Sutton Central Reservations at (514) 538-2646 can book you into anything from a private chalet to a small bed & breakfast.

Moderate

Auberge La Paimpolaise
This is a Sutton classic and a favorite of regulars to the area. Convenient slopeside location (it's almost part of the base area) and standard clean and comfortable motel-type rooms. A restaurant and bar are on-site. Rate $198 per person for 2 nights, including meals.
615 Maple St. Tel (514) 538-3213
Visa, MC, Amex, enRoute

Auberge Le Refuge
A small inn near the middle of town, it has only 12 rooms; they are comfortable and have great ambience. The personalized attention of the owners/operators is a welcome touch. Rates $35–$45 per person.
33 Maple St. Tel (514) 538-3802
Visa, MC

Hôtel Horizon
The oldest establishment in the area is starting to show signs of its age, but it's still a good spot given its convenience and price. Clean and basic motel-style rooms. A short drive to the slopes, and the only hotel in the area with an indoor pool. Also has a disco, games room and whirlpools. Rates $45–$60 per person.
297 Maple St. Tel (514) 538-3212
Visa, MC, Amex, Diners, enRoute

Val Sutton Condos
The newest and the most luxurious accommodation in the area is located up near Lift 5. (They do not have ski-to-your-door convenience; you must drive to

the base area, about five minutes away, or take the regular shuttle bus.) The units are in five clusters of 15 units each, and they are spiffy, with complete kitchens, fireplaces and one or two bedrooms. Many of the units can be connected with each other to increase occupancy. A good spot for large families and groups. Rates $27.50–$80 per person.

575 chemin Réal. Tel (514) 538-4444

Visa, MC, Amex

Village Archimède

A small collection of 40 tetrahedronal pre-fab condo pods elevated off the ground. Futuristic yet comfortable, they are within a short walk of the lifts. The units are well designed with the usual amenities. Rates $40–$55 per person.

582 Maple St. Tel (514) 538-3440

Visa, MC, Amex

Inexpensive

ESCO Lodge

A family-run hostel-type operation, there's nothing fancy about the place, but it has a friendly atmosphere and good basic rooms. Comes with a meal package only. Rates start at $195 for 5 nights.

435 Maple St. Tel (514) 538-2135

Visa, MC

La Capucine

A small inn run by the owners of ESCO, this place is cozy and comfortable, with 15 rooms that have that country inn feeling. Rates $40 per person including breakfast and dinner.

435 Maple St. Tel (514) 538-2135

Visa, MC

WHERE TO EAT

Expensive

Auberge à la Fontaine

The best dining in Sutton by far, and owners Lionel and Ninon go out of their way to make you feel at home. (In fact, they may rent you one of the upstairs bedrooms, the ultimate romantic hide-away for couples.) The food is French, with lots of specialty dishes such as duck and rabbit. The desserts are to die for. Our favorite spot for couples.

30 Principale sud. Tel 538-3045

Visa, MC

Moderate

Café Mocador

In a 150-year-old former stagecoach stop that has been converted into a number of intimate dining rooms, the Mocador is a Sutton tradition. Great atmosphere and a mixed menu of continental cuisine along with excellent service. A place you have to visit at least once on your trip to Sutton.

17 Principale nord. Tel 538-2426

Visa, MC, Amex

Café Santiago

Originally on Sutton's main street, Santiago is in new premises on the road up to the mountain. The menu remains the same, however: a good mix of continental dishes with a Spanish flair, and an emphasis on seafood.

212 Maple St. Tel 538-2660

Visa

Il Duetto

If you love Italian, this is the place to go. It's a small farmhouse restaurant just outside of town, and features typical Italian country cuisine. The pasta is excellent and the lamb is also a specialty.

227 chemin Academy-Élie. Tel 538-8239

Visa, MC, Amex

Le Refuge

A small dining room with great atmosphere and a continental menu with regular regional specials such as Brome Lake Duck.

In Auberge Le Refuge, 33 Maple St. Tel 538-3802

Visa, MC

Restaurant A&A Camille

A more traditional eatery featuring such North American staples as pizza, wings and ribs. Good for those with hearty appetites. Often features innovative all-you-can-eat specials such as lobster and Chinese stir-fry.

3 Principale sud. Tel 538-2456

Visa, MC, Amex

NIGHTLIFE

Sutton, it must be pointed out, does not rock. So it's a tad on the quiet side for the young and the relentless, but there are some spots where the après-ski is just right.

Loud and Lively

Auberge La Paimpolaise

This is the place to go for life after ski. The crowd is loud, freshly skied and in the mood for libations. There's music, ski movies, a house fondue and tons of good times. Later in the evening the tone is a little more subdued, but it's still a good spot for drinking and a little impromptu dancing.

615 Maple St. Tel 538-3213

Cedric's

In Knowlton about 10 mi (15 km) away, Cedric's is a first-class British pub that has rapidly become one of my favorites. It's more low-key than other pubs in town, and features darts. A good selection of British beers, and the place where the over-30 crowd is more likely to be found.

51 Lakeside, Knowlton. Tel 243-4100

Hôtel Camille

A good après-ski spot, Camille's is also the place to party later in the evening. There's a great stand-up bar and lots of loud dancing music with a place to shake it all loose. If you prefer to sip your beer in a more traditional environment, the Taverne in the same building is the place to go.

1 Principale sud. Tel 538-2201

Knowlton Pub

Knowlton is about 10 mi (15 km) away, and if your group has a designated chauffeur, the Pub is the place for those bent on drinking and depravity. It's loud, cheek-to-jowl, filled with a very young crowd, and the place where hormones flow like the beer. Just ask anyone in Knowlton for "the Pub."

267 Knowlton Rd, Knowlton. Tel 243-6862

Mellow

Auberge à la Fontaine

You can go directly to the bar in the Auberge after dinner in the dining room, but I recommend a walk about town before returning to the small (make that tiny) island bar in the middle of the dining room. It's just right for sitting, talking or playing backgammon, and so low-key I remember at least one occasion when Lionel, the owner, left us to serve ourselves when he was ready to call it a night.
33 Maple St. Tel 538-3802

Café Mocador

This is more for the espresso-sipping set. Kind of a Sartre feel to it, with quiet music (French, of course) and a variety of specialty coffees and liqueurs.
17 Principale nord. Tel 538-2426

Le Refuge

A late-night, coffee-sipping, liqueur-sampling, quiet-conversation type of place. Low-key music and a cozy atmosphere.
33 Maple St. Tel 538-3802

DIVERSIONS

A Touch of Art

The Galerie Arts Sutton is perfect for a quiet time of contemplation. The co-op gallery features regularly changing exhibitions by local artists, as well as special displays that feature the history and heritage of the region. First Saturday of every month they serve tea at 2 and 5. 7 rue de l'Académie. Call 538-2563.

Uplifting Experiences

For something a little uplifting, check out the "Aile Emoi" paragliding school near the mountain. You can take lessons, or go solo if you're an experienced flyer. Call Heinz Hefti at 538-2151 for info and reservations.

Soothing Moments

Even if you don't hit the trees while skiing Sutton's famed glade runs, you can still suffer from the aches and pains of a day on the slopes. Work those kinks out at the Centre de Relaxation Fiou, a small specialty massage parlor, with capable hands and reasonable prices. 14 Principale sud. Call 538-2633.

Chocolaterie Henquin

You owe it to yourself to try some of the best homemade chocolates that I've ever tasted. This tiny palace of pleasure is hard to find, but the Belgian chocolate specialties with homemade fillings are mouth-wateringly satisfying. Worth their weight in calories. 8 Principale sud. Call 538-0139.

MONT ORFORD

Box 248
Magog, Quebec
J1X 3W8
Tel (819) 843-6548

HOW TO GET THERE

By Car: Cross the St Lawrence from Montreal over the Champlain Bridge, then follow signs for Autoroute 10 to the Cantons de l'Est. It's about a 60-minute drive to Exit 115, which takes you to the base village at Mont Orford.

By Bus: Voyageur Bus (514-842-2281) has regular service from downtown Montreal.

Mont Orford, a three-mountain complex just 5 mi (8 km) from the town of Magog, has the third-highest vertical in Quebec. Although as a ski area it goes back more than half a century, it wasn't until the 1980s that substantial development was undertaken. The result is an ultra-modern complex that is efficient and well organized, but does lack that charm and ambience commonly associated with Quebec's major ski areas.

Not that it isn't blessed with some of the most striking topography in the Townships. The tallest peak in the Orford trio is Mont Orford, a heady 2,800 ft (854 m) high and commanding one of the most spectacular views in the region. To the south sits Lac Memphrémagog, a sinewy stretch of water that runs 30 mi (48 km) from Magog almost to the U.S. border. On a clear day you can see, farther south, the northern-most ridge of the Appalachians, and in all other directions the panorama is a mix of St Lawrence Valley Lowlands and the isolated peaks of the Townships.

The other two peaks of Orford are Mont Giroux, which rises 2,100 ft (640 m) directly above the base lodge area, and Mont Alfred DesRochers, 2,550 ft (777 m), on the western fringe of the resort. Thirty-three runs are spread over 180 acres (72 ha) and snowmaking covers 85 percent of the mountain. The vertical, at 1,772 (540 m), packs some punch, and the well-designed trail network provides not only good pitch but some of the longer runs in the area, including the 2 1/2-mi-long (4-km) La 4km, which twists and turns down along the top ridge of the mountain before dropping into the trees and back toward the lodge.

Most of the trails at Orford are the wide, high-speed cruising variety, and the shuttling of skiers from top to bottom is easily handled by the eight

MONT ORFORD— STATISTICALLY SPEAKING

Base Elevation:
1,000 ft (305 m)

Summit Elevation:
2,800 ft (854 m)

Vertical Drop:
1,772 ft (540 m)

Skiable Terrain:
180 acres (72 ha)

Number of Trails: 33

Longest Run: 2 1/2 mi (4 km)

Lifts & Capacity: 2 quads,
1 triple, 3 doubles, 2 surface;
11,200 skiers per hour

Lift Ticket: $5 per hour
Weekly: $135 (5 days)

Annual Snowfall:
200 in (510 cm)

No. Days Skiing 91–92: 141

Snowmaking: 85%

Terrain Mix:
N 36%, I 43%, E 21%

Snow Phone: 1-800-567-2772

lifts. A quad takes you from the village to the summit of Mont Giroux, from where you can zig and zag your way up and down all three mountains to get a feel for the variety of terrain.

At ground zero, the Orford base village is another model of efficiency and good design, a state-of-the-art condo village that affords ski-to-your-door convenience.

THE SKIING

There's no doubt that Orford is high-speed cruising territory—one regular I know calls it "401 skiing," a less than flattering reference to Canada's busiest highway. Another skiing comrade was more favorably impressed. A skiing machine who was weaned on the long runs and deep snow of western Canada, he was particularly smitten by the "long sweeping curves of Grande Coulee," and he positively raved about the "memorable and sensual sliding of La 4km."

While the full measure of Orford is gained by riding the white boulevards of speed, the resort is not without its steep pitches and rugged mogul runs. Take the Maxi, for instance, a steep, unrelenting pitch that throws up monster moguls and puts your skill—or lack of it—on display to all those riding in the quad chair overhead. Our western friend also finds sport in the "the drunken man's ravine," an unmarked and rocky little chute off the La 4km trail.

All told, the three peaks of Orford do offer some variety, and the interconnected layout of the three peaks makes it a good spot for families and groups of varying abilities.

One final point about Orford: this is an exposed piece of geography, and when the wind bears down from the north or the east it can be *cold*. This is not the place to be caught without neck warmers and goggles.

HOW TO SKI MONT ORFORD

Novices

Ride the Quatuor Chair from the bottom of Mont Giroux and stick to runs like Gagnon, Familiale and Petite Coulee. From the top of Mont Orford, try the longest run on the mountain, La 4km.

Intermediates

There's a quartet of good, fast-paced intermediate trails off the summit of Mont Alfred DesRochers, including Cascades, Grand Allée and Ookpic. From the top of Mont Giroux try Slalom.

Experts

Mont Orford has the steepest runs at the resort, among them Trois-Ruisseaux, and some nasty steep mogul pitches like L'Entre-Deux and Diversion.

WHERE TO STAY

There's no shortage of accommodation in the region: there are more than 5,000 beds within a 10-mile radius. It ranges from the on-mountain condo complexes to the smaller hotels and motels of nearby Magog, or the luxury auberges and inns in neighboring Hatley and Ayer's Cliff.

All accommodation can be arranged through the Mont Orford Reservation Bureau at (819) 843-2744.

Expensive

Auberge Estrimont

Halfway between Mont Orford and Lac Memphrémagog, this collection of 82 condo suites is one of my favorites. Units include fireplace, balcony and a spectacular view. Also, one of the few facilities in the area with a fully equipped health club, including indoor pool. Rates $152–$175 per person for 2 days with meals.

44 ave de l'Auberge, Magog. Tel (819) 843-1616

Visa, MC, Amex

Le Chéribourg

A luxury collection of 97 units, about five minutes from the slopes. Units range from one to three bedrooms and have all the usual amenities; some have

fireplaces. A pretty setting, close to the great cross-country skiing of Orford Provincial Park. Has a dining room and bar. Rates $115–$135 per person for 2 nights with meals.
2603 Road 141 North, Magog. Tel (819) 843-3308
Visa, MC, Amex

Le Village Mont Orford
There's nothing more convenient than this condo village just 200 yards from the lifts. A variety of luxury units with one to three bedrooms; all have fireplace and balcony and some have extras like dishwasher and microwave. Rates $75–$123 per person.
5015 chemin de Parc, Magog. Tel (819) 847-2662, toll-free (Ontario, Quebec, Maritimes, U.S.) 1-800-567-7315
Visa, MC, Amex

Moderate
The following trio of inns not only offer fine accommodation but actually link together in an all-inclusive package for cross-country skiers. The trail runs for 22 mi (35 km), and guests stop over at each inn. (See "Diversions" for details.) Alpine skiers can also stay at these special country inns.

Auberge Hatley
A 25-room inn, with luxury suites (some with whirlpools) and also some regular rooms. All feature antique furnishings. Rates $100–$245 per person with meals.
Route 108, North Hatley. Tel (819) 842-2451
Visa, MC

Hovey Manor
A beautiful collection of 36 suites in an estate setting modeled after the Virginia home of George Washington. Rooms are comfortable and tastefully furnished with antiques, and the setting is spectacular. Rates $140–$175 per person with meals.
Chemin Hovey, North Hatley. Tel (819) 842-2421
Visa, MC, Amex

MONT ORFORD—
FIVE 5-STAR FAVORITES

Best Run for Vertical
Trois-Ruisseaux

Best Overall Run
Grande Coulee

Best Restaurant
Chez Jean Pierre

Best Nightclub/Bar
La Lanterne

Best Accommodation
Le Chéribourg
  Jamie Doran, Mont Orford

Ripplecove Inn
A 12-acre (5-ha) lakeside estate with 11 rooms and seven chalets, which include fireplaces. A stunning location on the shores of Lake Massawippi, where you can skate and cross-country ski. Rates $92–$140 with meals.
700 rue Ripplecove, Ayer's Cliff. Tel (819) 838-4296
Visa, MC, Amex

Inexpensive
Nearby Magog is your best bet for basic motel-type accommodation.

Motel de la Pente Douce
Thirty comfortable, clean rooms, 13 with efficiency kitchens. Rate $49 double occupancy.
1787 Route 141 nord. Tel (819) 843-1234
Visa, MC, Amex

Motel du Ranch
Twelve basic rooms, starting at $45 per person.
3005 chemin Miletta, Magog. Tel (819) 847-4091
Visa, MC, Amex

WHERE TO EAT
Expensive
Auberge Estrimont
An excellent hotel dining room serving smoked trout, lamb and other local specialties.
44 ave de l'Auberge, Magog. Tel 843-1616
Visa, MC, enRoute

Le Chéribourg
An excellent dining room that has won several awards. Some of the specialties include stuffed breast of duck, rack of lamb and flambé pepper

steak. Expensive, but worth it. Reservations recommended.
2603 Road 141 North, Magog. Tel 843-3308
Visa, MC, Amex

Moderate
Chez Benito
A mix of Italian dishes such as veal and pasta, with a good selection of local specialties including Brome Lake duck.
20 rue Merry sud, Magog. Tel 843-9361
Visa, MC, Amex

Chez Jean Pierre
A delightful little restaurant with checkered tablecloths and an array of flambé dishes. It has mostly French cuisine with some interesting local touches.
112 rue Principale ouest, Magog. Tel 843-8166
Visa, MC

Inexpensive
Les Trois Marmites
An excellent restaurant for families or those on a budget. The portions are large, and the roast beef buffet is especially popular.
475 rue Principale ouest, Magog. Tel 843-4448
Visa, MC, Amex

NIGHTLIFE
Loud and Lively
La Grosse Pomme
A crazy place in downtown Magog that features everything from movies to disco dancing. It's large, multi-leveled, filled with a mostly young crowd, and it rocks until the small hours.
270 rue Principale ouest. Tel 843-9365

La Lanterne
A good spot to head to for life after ski. The crowd is a good mix, and the noise level is tolerable. Later on the dance music starts, and the action changes pace without skipping a beat. Also a good spot for dinner.
70 du Lac, Magog. Tel 843-7205

MONT ORFORD—USEFUL
TELEPHONE NUMBERS
(area code 819)

Towing 843-6262

Provedenca Hospital
843-3381

Police 564-1212

Oui Ski Bar

The place for after-ski action right at the mountain. It gets crowded early, and many folks stay till the end, around midnight. Usually has live entertainment in the form of chansonniers, and reckless patrons are often keen to display their own musical talents. The hot buttered rum is a crowd-pleaser.

In Mont Orford's main lodge, at the bottom of the hill

Mellow

For quieter moments after dinner your best bets are the various lounges in the hotel complexes such as Auberge Estrimont and Chéribourg.

DIVERSIONS

A Tour of Three

The cross-country ski tour that links the three inns listed in "Where to Stay/Moderate" is one of two such networks in Canada. The Skiwippi package runs for 22 mi (35 km) between Ayer's Cliff and North Hatley. Calories expended on the trail are quickly replaced by sumptuous dining at each overnight stop. (Your luggage is moved for you.) The three-day package, including accommodation, food and luggage transfer, is a real deal at $360 per person. For more information write to Auberge Hatley, C.P. 330, North Hatley, P.Q. J0B 2C0, or call (819) 838-4296.

QUEBEC CITY

HOW TO GET THERE
By Plane: Quebec City Airport has connecting flights from Montreal and other major centers via Air Canada, Air Alliance, Air-Québec Métro and Northwest.

By Car: From Montreal take Henry IV Autoroute (Hwy 20) to Hwy 40 east. Follow Hwy 40 and take the exit for Hwy 138 east, to Beaupré, then Hwy 360 to Mont Ste-Anne.

By Train: Via Rail and Amtrak run to Montreal, with connections to Quebec City.

No city in North America has an affection for winter like Quebec City. From the madness of the annual winter carnival—a somewhat overrated and highly commercialized drunk-fest—to the solitude of gliding on cross-country skis across the historic Plains of Abraham, there's no other place where the games of snow and ice are so much a part of life.

Spreading north and east from the shores of the St Lawrence River, the snowy playgrounds yield more than 625 mi (1000 km) of groomed cross-country trails and two of the most modern and best-run alpine ski resorts in eastern Canada. They reap the bounty of a rolling extension of the Laurentian mountains and frequent snowfalls, and annually draw more than a million skiers to their slopes.

The modernity of the resorts is in distinct contrast to historic Quebec City, but the captivating charm of the largest walled city north of Mexico is one reason Mont Ste-Anne and Stoneham warrant their place among the best resorts in Canada.

MONT STE-ANNE

Box 400
Beaupré, Quebec
G0A 1E0
Tel (418) 827-4561

HOW TO GET THERE

By Car: Mont Ste-Anne is 25 mi (40 km) northeast of Quebec City. From the airport follow Hwy 40 north of the city, then take Hwy 138 along the north shore of the St Lawrence River to the town of Beaupré. Make a sharp left turn on to Hwy 360 and follow the signs for St-Féréol-les-Neiges.

From Montreal it's about a 3 1/2-hour drive (180 mi/ 290 km) via Autoroute 20 to Hwy 40.

By Bus: Regular shuttle bus services leave from all major Quebec City hotels. Voyageur and Greyhound bus lines run a regular service from the Quebec City main bus terminal.

The development of Mont Ste-Anne over the past decade has been nothing short of spectacular. It has grown from a little-known backwater resort on the outskirts of one of the prettiest cites on the continent to a major-league destination with state-of-the-art covered lifts, computerized snowmaking, the highest and longest lighted trails in the east and a ski season that rivals the perennial champion of the first-to-open-last-to-close contest, Vermont's Killington.

Mont Ste-Anne is now the biggest and most modern ski resort in eastern Canada, and draws more skiers annually than any Canadian resort except Whistler. The more than $35 million that has been spent since the mid-1980s has seen the base area grow into a bustling little village of hotels, condos, boutiques and a convention center. On the mountain it has produced a brand-new eight-passenger gondola, three quad chairs, 18 new trails and a snowmaking system that covers 85 percent oi the skiing terrain.

The three-sided mountain has the second-highest vertical in the east, with more than 400 acres (160 ha) of skiable terrain and 50 trails. Nearby, the small communities of Ste-Anne-de-Beaupré and St-Féréol-les-Neiges have thrived accordingly, and a flourishing nest of restaurants and small auberges have sprung up to accommodate the crowds. In short, everything has come together into a remarkably efficient package of good skiing, varied accommodation and, of course, the indisputable allure of Quebec City.

THE SKIING

Regulars to Mont Ste-Anne will tell you that the best way to ski the mountain is to follow the sun. That means starting on the south side in the morning, moving over to the north side after lunch and maybe

Base Elevation:
575 ft (175 m)

Summit Elevation:
2,625 ft (800 m)

Vertical Drop:
2,050 ft (625 m)

Skiable Terrain:
400 acres (160 ha)

Number of Trails: 50

Longest Run: 3 mi (5 km)

Lifts & Capacity: 1 gondola,
3 quads, 1 triple, 2 doubles;
17,761 skiers per hour

Daily Lift Ticket: $38
Weekly: $167

Annual Snowfall:
148 in (375 cm)

No. Days Skiing 91–92: 170

Snowmaking: 85%

Terrain Mix:
N 22%, I 48%, E 30%

Snow Phone: 827-5727

finishing up the day on the west face. Great in theory, but in practice the sun is often in short supply on this mountain—partly because of the typical winter storms that blow through the region, and partly because of the low clouds that hug the shoreline of the St Lawrence River.

Sun or no sun, it still makes sense to follow that route. The south face of the resort has the most vertical and the greatest concentration of runs. (It also has the fastest way to the summit, via the eight-passenger gondola.) And with its long runs, Ste-Anne is a mountain to be skied from top to bottom. La Beaupré and Le Gros Vallon are two long, winding descents that start off tight among the trees then widen out as they curve around the mid-section of the mountain and afford a dazzling view of the St Lawrence far below. At the eastern end of the ridge is another pair of intermediate cruisers that tend to be the busiest runs on the south side, L'Express and La Tourmente.

The toughest runs at Ste-Anne are also on the south face, including La Crête, which is accessible via the summit catwalk to the west of the gondola. It's steep, with some sections narrow and packed with moguls, and it's one of the longest runs at the area. It's also the site of the women's World Cup downhill when the "white circus" is in town.

The north side of the mountain, served by one high-speed quad, has mostly intermediate runs, and it's a good place to head for when the brisk, icy winds are blowing up from the river. And for my money there's no place better to enjoy the sun than the deck area at the Refuge de Nord, a cozy day lodge that serves up homemade crepes with maple syrup; don't ski Mont Ste-Anne without enjoying this classic French-Canadian treat. And if the sun isn't shining, the warm, steamy ambience is a satisfying and filling respite from the weather.

The west side of the mountain also features mostly intermediate cruising runs, and though it's served only by a T-bar, the crowds tend to stick to the other two faces, and that means relatively short lineups.

At the end of the day, there's nothing better than a long, easy cruise down to the après-ski action, and if your legs can still hack it, try 1-B from the summit; it's a little steep at first, but by mid-mountain it flattens out just a tad and gives you a high-adrenaline charge that helps build an appetite. If your ego screams yes but your legs plead no, choose Pichard for your last run; it takes a circuitous 2-mi (3-km) cruise down to the bottom.

HOW TO SKI MONT STE-ANNE

Novices

Stick to the two quad chairs on the west side of the resort; they carry you to the long novice runs that sweep down the western flank. In the afternoon, the right-hand runs on the north side give you a chance to enjoy the relative solitude of this part of the mountain.

Intermediates

Head for the two quad chairs that service the western side of the ridge for some warm-up runs, then cut back to the gondola for some fast and steep cruising. In the afternoon, the north side is your best friend, and at the end of the day try either La Crête or 1-B for a fast run down.

Experts

Take the gondola to the summit, then follow the catwalk over to the top of the triple chair and take a crack at 1 and 1-B. Also try La Gondoleuse, the run immediately under the gondola. After those warm-up runs, take one of 2-A or 2-B, depending on your feelings about moguls; they are the toughest and steepest runs on the mountain.

WHERE TO STAY

Even though I prefer staying on or near the mountain at almost any ski resort, Mont Ste-Anne is one place where that inclination is often waived, because of the charms of nearby Quebec City. Not that there aren't some fine spots to bed down in near the resort, but the lure of Quebec is sufficient to recommend it as an entirely agreeable alternative.

Keep in mind that Quebec City is a 40-minute drive from the mountain, and in some weather the drive can be tricky. If you stay on the mountain and head to the city for nightlife, a designated driver is a must.

All accommodation can be booked through Reservotel, the central reservation system. Call toll-free (U.S. & Canada) 1-800-463-1568.

Expensive
Hôtel Château Mont Ste-Anne
This hotel is exactly what a ski resort hotel should be. Large rooms, with lofts and kitchens, a great lobby bar with après-ski fondues and evening entertainment, plus large, wide ramps and stairways ideal for clomping up and down in ski boots, and ski-to-your-back-door convenience. (My only complaint is the slow elevators.) Rates $133–$218 per person including lift ticket.
500 boul Beau-Pré, Beaupré. Tel (418) 827-5211, toll-free (U.S. & Canada) 1-800-463-4467
Visa, MC, Amex, Diners, enRoute

Hôtel Val des Neiges
A great spot opposite the ski slopes, it has 110 rooms of various sizes, including some with fireplace, dining room and jacuzzi. Also has a great sports center with pool, sauna, hot tubs, whirlpool and exercise rooms. Rates $90–$125 per person including meals and lift ticket.
201 rue Val des Neiges, Beaupré. Tel (418) 827-5711, toll-free (Canada) 1-800-463-5250
Visa, MC, Amex, enRoute, Discover

Moderate
Chalets Mont Ste-Anne
A pleasant little chalet complex that has one- through five-bedroom units. A good choice for families and large groups, and for those who like to entertain their friends at home. Rates $104–$124 per unit.
Right at the bottom of the slopes. Tel (418) 827-5776, toll-free (Canada) 1-800-463-4467
Visa, MC, Amex

Chalets Montmorency
I have to confess a special weakness for the Chalets Montmorency; I've watched it grow from an eight-unit complex to its current 32-unit size. The chalets are spacious, convenient (just 800 yards to the hill) and great for large groups and families. Also has an indoor pool and spa facility. Rates $45–$65 per person.
1768 Royale, St-Féréol-les-Neiges. Tel (418) 826-2600, toll-free (Canada & U.S.) 1-800-463-2612
Visa, MC, Diners

Inexpensive
Auberge Chez Albert
Albert makes great pizza, and he also has 10 nifty motel units within easy walking distance of the mountain. They don't come fully dressed, but they are comfortable and almost brand-new. A good spot, and you can always step next door for Albert's specialty (see "Where to Eat"). Rates $40–$55.
1805 boul des Neiges, St-Féréol-les-Neiges. Tel (418) 826-2184
Visa, MC

L'Aventure
Just half a mile (1 km) from the resort, L'Aventure is one of my new favorites in the area. It has just nine rooms, and each is well appointed and spacious. Amenities include bar discotheque, dining room and outdoor pool. Rates $59–$99 per room.
355 rue Dupont. Tel (418) 827-5748
Visa, MC

La Maison Baker
Maison Baker is a great bed & breakfast (and an excellent restaurant). There are just eight rooms, all cozy and furnished with antiques. About 5 mi (8 km) from the mountain. Rates $35–$55.
8790 ave Royale, Château Richer. Tel (418) 824-4478
Visa, MC

IN QUEBEC CITY

Expensive

Château Frontenac

There's no place that epitomizes the style and heritage of Quebec City quite like the Château Frontenac. Perched high above the St Lawrence River, overlooking the port and the old town of Quebec City, the fortress-like Château is a mélange of turrets and parapets. Inside it's all style and elegance, from the uniformed doormen to the fur-clad guests. Many of the rooms have been recently renovated (although some remain despairingly small, some with single beds, no less). Trappings include numerous bars, lounges and restaurants, a shopping arcade and health club facilities. Rates $120–$180.

1 rue des Carrières. Tel (418) 692-3861, toll-free (U.S.) 1-800-828-7447, (Ontario) 1-800-268-9420, (other provinces) 1-800-268-9411

Visa, MC, Amex, enRoute

Loews Le Concorde

The modern counterpoint to the Château, Le Concorde sits just outside the walls of the old city high above the Plains of Abraham. The rooms are large and comfortable, the view spectacular, and the location is convenient to the city's trendiest nightlife. Also has a hot disco, health club and a revolving restaurant on top. Rates $99–$185.

1225 Place Montcalm. Tel (418) 647-2222, toll-free (Quebec, Ontario, Maritimes) 1-800-463-5256, (western Canada & U.S.) 1-800-223-0888

Visa, MC, Amex, enRoute

WHERE TO EAT

Expensive

La Bécassine

If you enjoy game dishes, this restaurant, which is tucked away alongside the fast-food joints and strip plazas on the highway up to Mont Ste-Anne, is not to be missed. Its specialty is almost anything except domestic livestock. Roast duckling with maple syrup is one of my favorites, and goose, rabbit, quail, country lamb and reindeer are other seasonal specialties.

9341 boul Ste-Anne. Tel 827-4798

Visa, MC, Amex

La Camarine

This is haute-cuisine with a nouvelle twist, and one of the best dining experiences in the area. There's a whole raft of daily specials, ranging from lamb to duck, with some of the most memorable sauces to accompany them. The menu changes frequently, so enjoying the same dish twice is difficult, but I do remember fondly a fine bouillabaisse, excellent rabbit and fantastic lobster. Also has an excellent wine list, and if you don't wish to spring megadollars for the whole bottle you can sip in the wine bar downstairs. Reservations recommended.

42 Côte Ste-Anne, Beaupré. Tel 827-5566

Visa, MC

La Maison Baker

If you want ambience and fine dining with a distinctive flair, don't miss La Maison Baker. The menu is an eclectic mix of traditional Quebecois specialties and haute-cuisine. It's also served with great flair. Reservations recommended. About 10 minutes east of Mont Ste-Anne.

8790 ave Royale, Château Richer. Tel 824-4478

Visa, MC

Moderate

Chez Albert

Right opposite the Chalets Montmorency, Albert serves up a mean designer pizza from huge open-hearth ovens. He also does a nice job on the pasta dishes, and the salads are a meal in themselves.

1768 ave Royale, St-Féréol-les-Neiges. Tel 826-2184

Visa, MC, Diners

Chez Colette

This used to be a favorite of the locals until the tourists discovered it. It serves up some great meals accompanied by a great view out over the St Lawrence. A good offering of traditional Quebecois fare. I heartily recommend the bouillabaisse.

2190 ave Royale, St-Féréol-les-Neiges. Tel 826-2944

Visa, MC

Inexpensive

About 5 mi (8 km) down from Mont Ste-Anne there's a gaudy strip of neon lights and fast-food eateries. If quantity, simplicity and price are your primary concerns, this area offers you everything from burgers to barbecue chicken to poutin, a local concoction of french-fries, gravy and cheese curds.

IN QUEBEC CITY

Here are my recommendations—no easy task for a city with more than 300 restaurants, bistros and cafés!

Expensive

Aux Anciens Canadiens

You *have* to eat here. This lovely red and white brick structure is the oldest house in Quebec City. Built in 1675, it remains much as it was then, with thick fieldstone walls and a steep roof. The menu is a mixture of some contemporary dishes—salmon pie, lamb, veal, rabbit—and more typical Quebecois specialties such as tourtière and fèves au lard. Try the maple sugar pie.

34 rue St Louis. Tel 692-1627

Visa, MC, Amex, enRoute

Gambrinus

Another favorite. The menu is the reason—it's a refreshing mix of Italian and French. Pasta and veal are two specialties, but there's also a good rack of lamb and some excellent steaks. Within walking distance of the Château Frontenac. Reservations recommended.

15 rue du Fort. Tel 692-5144

Visa, MC, Amex, enRoute

Le Marie-Clarisse

I like this cozy little dining room, with its fieldstone fireplace and wood floors, and also because it serves some of the freshest fish dishes anywhere. There are usually at least four daily fish specials, and they are invariably cooked with some unusual accompaniments. The shark is excellent. Reservations recommended.

12 rue Petit Champlain. Tel 692-0857

Visa, MC, Amex, Diners, enRoute

Le St-Amour

A good varied menu of everyday favorites done up in a creative and tantalizing fashion. The range of entrees runs from fish—trout, salmon, dore and lobster—to red meat—lamb, filet mignon—and every dish is perfect. A superb wine list is also reason enough to visit this spot. Reservations recommended.

48 rue Ste-Ursule. Tel 694-0667

Visa, MC, Amex, enRoute

Serge Bruyère

This restaurant has been ranked one of the finest, if not *the* finest, in Canada. My confirmation can come only from several spectacular meals enjoyed there, at someone else's expense. The tab is large, but the satisfaction immense. The menu is vast. I particularly enjoyed the terrine of rabbit, though everything from the soups and salads to the desserts is near perfect. If a $200 dinner tab is not your style, consider lunch; it's a whole lot cheaper, and the food is just as superb. Reservations a must.

1200 rue St-Jean. Tel 694-0618

Visa, MC, Amex

Moderate

To my mind there's no better way to soak up the ambience of Quebec City than to enjoy a leisurely light meal at one of the many traditional cafés. You can linger for hours over a salad and a steaming bowl of soup or some local specialties. Here are some of my favorite spots for light dining and great people watching.

Café Millefeuille

This charming spot features a vegetarian menu with a good choice of salads, some excellent cheese plates and other non-meat specialties such as an excellent vegetable strudel. Desserts are good, and the selection of fine ports is second to none.

32 rue Ste-Angèle. Tel 692-2147

Visa, MC

Chez Temporal

A good spot for homemade soups, innovative salads and a variety of quiches. Also serves an excellent croque monsieur and some novel baguette sandwiches.

25 rue Couillard. No telephone.

No cards

The Lapin Saute
Rabbit is the specialty here—a different dish each day of the week—but there's also a good selection of such staples as croque monsieur, homemade soups and interesting hamburgers—try the blue cheese special. The fudge cake is the most decadent thing I've ever tasted.
52 rue Petit Champlain. Tel 692-5325
Visa, MC, Amex, enRoute

NIGHTLIFE
Downtown Quebec City has no shortage of nightlife and entertainment. Check out the Quartier du Petit-Champlain, immediately below the Château Frontenac on the Terrasse Dufferin, or take the escalier Casse-Cou (the breakneck staircase) down to the boutiques, restaurants and bistros that line the narrow streets in this oldest section of the city.

If you're looking for more contemporary action, head for the Grande Allée just outside the stone gates of the old town up near Loews Le Concorde. This street is one of the city's busiest thoroughfares, and is often referred to as the Champs-Elysée of Quebec. On both sides of the street there are numerous bars, restaurants, discotheques and nightclubs—many of which stay open until 4 a.m.

Loud and Lively
Immediately after skiing head for the day lodge adjacent to the Château Mont Ste-Anne. The upstairs Chouette bar is a wild and happening place, with extra-loud music, free-flowing beer and free-form dancing. It's loud, smoky and filled with steaming bodies.
Mont Ste-Anne Resort. Tel 827-5461

L'Aventure
This is my favorite new place at Mont Ste-Anne. About half a mile (1 km) from the resort on the road running down from the mountain, it's a two-story old style taverne, with a combination dining room/bar that serves up some good pizza and pasta as well some good après-ski fun. The second floor has pool tables and disco action later in the evening. It's the spot locals head for, so bring along your best French and meet some new friends.
355 rue Dupont. Tel 827-3121

**MONT STE-ANNE—
FIVE 5-STAR FAVORITES**

Best Run for Vertical
Familiale

Best Overall Run
Grosvallon

Best Restaurant
La Camarine

Best Nightclub/Bar
L'Aventure

Best Accommodation
Hôtel Château Mont Ste-
Anne
*Julie Gagnon,
Mont Ste-Anne*

**MONT STE-ANNE—USEFUL
TELEPHONE NUMBERS**
(area code 418)

Taxi Ste-Anne 827-2330

Taxi Tremblay 827-5160

Les Terrasses

The over-30 crowd tends to head for this après-ski spot on the second floor of the new day lodge near the covered quad chair. The music is a little more temperate, the crowd a little quieter, and it's more of a spot to sit and talk than to move around and boogie.

Mont Ste-Anne Resort. Tel 827-5461

DIVERSIONS
Ski du Fond

The Parc du Mont Ste-Anne is a fantastic place for a little skinny skiing, especially when the alpine slopes are crowded. The network of 133 mi (214 km) is the largest in Canada, and it winds through some spectacular wooded areas to the west of the alpine ski area. There are also 62 mi (100 km) of trails for the skaters and eight warming huts along the network. For those who want to linger overnight, the Auberge du Fondeur, a 10-room lodge in the heart of the park, costs between $30–$40 per person including breakfast. (For more information call 418-827-4561.) Alpine skiers who buy a five-day lift pass get free skiing at the nordic center.

Sleigh Rides

A great après-ski or après-dinner activity is a sleigh ride through the snow-covered streets and fields of Mont Ste-Anne or nearby St-Féréol. You can join a group or gather your own. Call 827-4561.

SKI STONEHAM

1420 ave du Hibou
Stoneham, Quebec
G0A 4P0
Tel (418) 848-2411

HOW TO GET THERE

By Car: From Montreal, take either Autoroute 20 on the south shore of the St Lawrence, or Autoroute 40 on the north shore. Both connect with Hwy 73 north across the top of Quebec City, which takes you to Hwy 175 north to the Stoneham exit. From downtown Quebec City, take Hwy 440 west to Hwy 73, then north to Hwy 175 and the Stoneham exit. The drive from Montreal takes about 2 1/2 hours, from downtown Quebec City about 25 minutes.

By Bus: Greyhound Bus Lines runs regular service from downtown Quebec City to the resort.

Just 25 minutes from downtown Quebec City, Stoneham is a spectacularly designed modern resort that has thrived despite existing in the shadow of nearby Mont Ste-Anne. While that larger, louder neighbor was indulging in a mega-million-dollar spending spree and attracting masses from all over the continent, Stoneham was quietly and successfully building a loyal clientele that relishes its more stylish and service-oriented approach. At Ste-Anne they can move the masses up the mountain, but at Stoneham they meet you at the parking lot and help unload your skies. For those who like attention to detail and the feel of a private club, Stoneham is your best bet in the Quebec City region.

The beautifully designed base area has a hotel, plus 120 condo units spread across the property, with 60 of the units cleverly placed on the lower part of the trails at the south end of the resort. All the accommodation is within walking distance of the lifts, and from the slopeside condos you have ski-in/ski-out convenience.

There's also a picturesque quality to Stoneham. It's situated in a horseshoe-shaped valley with its mountain ridge of six peaks forming an outdoor amphitheatre that acts as a natural snow trap and wind buffer. Lac Beauport lies to the south, and from any of the area's peaks you have a marvelous view of the Quebec City skyline.

THE SKIING

There's good skiing at Stoneham, with an interesting mix of terrain, generally excellent snow conditions, consistent grooming and an efficient lift system. There are six mountains on the Stoneham property, though only four are so far developed for skiing. The mountains are identified by number, and the trails on each are given numbers. Trails 1–7 are on

Base Elevation:
530 ft (162 m)

Summit Elevation:
1,950 ft (595 m)

Vertical Drop:
1,420 ft (433 m)

Skiable Terrain:
300 acres (120 ha)

Number of Trails: 25

Longest Run: 2.1 mi (3.4 km)

Lifts & Capacity: 4 quads,
2 doubles, 4 surface lifts;
9,600 skiers per hour

Daily Lift Ticket: $28
Weekly: $107 (5 days)

Annual Snowfall:
160 in (400 cm)

No. Days Skiing 91–92: 143

Snowmaking: 92%

Terrain Mix:
N 30%, I 40%, E 30%

Snow Phone: 848-2415

Mountain #1; trails 8–19 are on Mountain #2, and trails 40–46 are on Mountain #4. (Mountain #6 is for snowboarders only, and Mountains #3 and #5 are still to be developed.)

There are about 300 acres (120 ha) of skiable terrain at the resort and 25 trails. The 1,420 ft (433 m) of vertical may not appear that substantial in light of some of Quebec's larger ski areas, but it is sufficient to keep all but hard-core vertical junkies happy, and good enough to run World Cup races on. In December 1992, Stoneham will host two men's World Cup races, a slalom and a giant slalom, and if the racers of the "white circus" find it challenging, so should the rest of us.

HOW TO SKI STONEHAM
Novices
Start on Mountain #1, on either trail 2 or 6, which is the longest run at the resort. Both are easy sliders. Next head over to Mountain #2 and try trail 19. About halfway down connect with 6; combined, they give you a good long run with a great view of the valley.

Intermediates
Start off on Mountain #1 and take a good giant slalom cruise down trail 7. After that, head for Mountain #2 and hit trail 8, which curves around the top half of the peak. At mid-mountain continue on 7 for full-speed running, or cut hard left and take the bumpy route down on 7B. Also try the straight-shot down 9, but watch out if you're carrying too much speed because at mid-mountain it turns into four narrow black diamond options: 9, 9B, 9C and 9D. On Mountain #4, try run 41 for a long cruise to the bottom.

Best Run for Vertical
Trail 45

Best Overall Run
Trail 41

Best Restaurant
Restaurant Praline

Best Bar/Nightclub
Pub St-Emond

Best Accommodation
Condominiums Stoneham
Denys Legare, Stoneham

STONEHAM—USEFUL
TELEPHONE NUMBERS
(area code 418)

Ski Bus (Mont Ste-Anne &
Stoneham) 653-9722

Taxi Quebec 525-8123

Road Conditions 643-6830

Experts

On Mountain #1, take a warm-up on the steep upper part of runs 1 or 1B. Trail 1 cuts through the trees, then widens out about halfway down; 1B is a little wider up top, then intersects with 1. Mountain #4 is where you'll have the most fun. Trails 44 and 46 are double black diamond affairs that have great pitch (and maximum vertical) at the top, then a long, winding, high-speed run out to the bottom. These are the runs that the World Cup races are staged on.

WHERE TO STAY

There are slopeside hotels and condos at Stoneham, and they are eminently satisfactory.

Of course the hundreds of hotels, inns and lodges of Quebec City are also nearby. See "Where to Stay/In Quebec City" under Mont Ste-Anne.

All can be booked through Stoneham's Central Reservations number, (418) 848-2411, toll-free (Canada) 1-800-463-6888.

Expensive

Condominiums Stoneham

If you prefer a little more space and the opportunity to prepare your own meals, the condos at Stoneham are a good bet. They are some of the best on-slope accommodation I've stayed at in eastern Canada. The 120 units range from studios to 4-bedrooms, which sleep eight. Sixty of them are right at the bottom of the lifts, and the other 60 are on the side of trail 41. The furnishings are top quality, and each unit is completely equipped with fireplace, private balcony, kitchen and washer-dryer. Minimum 2-night stay. Rates $198–$270 (for a studio for 2 nights); $376–$638 (for a 4-bedroom for 2 nights). 1420 ave du Hibou. Tel (418) 848-2411, toll-free (Canada) 1-800-463-6888
Visa, MC

Hôtel Stoneham
Like all things at Stoneham, this is a well-built, stylish and luxurious facility. Has 60 large rooms, most with two double beds and a great view of the mountain. Ski-in/ski-out access. Rates $73–$110 per person.
1440 ave du Hibou. Tel (418) 848-2000/2411, toll-free (Canada) 1-800-463-6888
Visa, MC

Moderate
Hôtel Faubourg Stoneham
It's not quite slopeside, but it's the next best thing—just two minutes down the road. It's a first-rate facility with 44 rooms, most with two double beds. Also has a dining room and lounge. Rates $60–$100 per person.
825 ave du Hibou. Tel (418) 848-1333
Visa, MC

WHERE TO EAT
See also "Where to Eat/In Quebec City" under Mont Ste-Anne.

Expensive
Restaurant Praline
This is the best dining on the mountain. The menu is continental, with table d'hôte specials each day. The specialty is fish, though the veal dishes are also highly recommended. Elegant but not pretentious. Room for about 100, so reservations are necessary on weekends.
In the base lodge, 1420 ave du Hibou. Tel 848-2411
Visa, MC

Moderate
Pâtes Montagne
This casual dining spot puts the emphasis on pasta dishes and pizza. Different specials daily, and an enjoyable atmosphere.
In the Hôtel Stoneham, 1440 ave du Hibou. Tel 848-3811
Visa, MC

NIGHTLIFE
Downtown Quebec City has all the nightlife you could wish for. Check out the

old town, or the Grande Allée, where most of the discos, bars and nightclubs are clustered. If you're staying at the mountain, here are two good choices close to home.

Four Fire Place Bar
Don't ask for this by its given name—it'll immediately identify you as a tourist. They like to keep things simple at Stoneham, hence this is The Bar (and the St-Emond is The Pub). It's a good après-ski hang-out, though it's later on that it really cooks when the disco heats up. There's a mix of recorded music and live bands, and lots of dancing.
In the base lodge, 1420 ave du Hibou. Tel 848-2411

Pub St-Emond
A traditional pub with lots of immediate après-ski action, then a more relaxed pace later in the evening. Lots of traditional pub games, a good selection of imported beers and always a convivial crowd.
In the Hôtel Stoneham, 1440 ave du Hibou. Tel 848-2000

DIVERSIONS
Quebec City with all its charms is a major diversion for anyone, but there's plenty to divert one slopeside at Stoneham. There's a great skating rink, on the tennis courts at the base of trail 1. There's also organized sleigh rides and of course night skiing. (In fact, Stoneham has the largest night skiing system in Canada, with two-thirds of its total terrain under the lights.)

10 MORE SKI RESORTS THAT RATE A VISIT

When I made the final selection for the 20 resorts included in this book there were many contenders that just could not be squeezed into the top 20. That doesn't make them any less worthy of your visit. Here are 10 that I feel warrant an honorable mention.

MARBLE MOUNTAIN

Box 252

Steady Brook, Newfoundland

A2H 2N2

Tel (709) 634-2160

If hospitality was the sole criterion for assessing a ski resort, Newfoundland's Marble Mountain would be number one. However, other attributes make this eastern-most resort so remarkable: 1,600 ft (490 m) of vertical, 200 in (500 cm) of snow annually, 128 acres (51 ha) of terrain and a long run of 3 mi (4.8 km). And then there's that reputation for "down-home" hospitality, a genuine friendliness that goes hand in hand with some of the purest traditional folk music in North America. It's special, it's growing, and it's some of the best skiing east of the Rockies.

MONT FARLAGNE

Box 61

Edmundston, New Brunswick

E3V 3K7

Tel (506) 735-8401

New Brunswick is not the first place that comes to mind when you think about ski areas, but 2 mi (3 km) north of Edmunston is Mont Farlagne, a fine resort that draws skiers from Maine, Quebec and Atlantic Canada. It's not big—just 17 runs—but it is fun, and supremely well organized on the après-ski side of things. On the slopes, the vertical is about 600 ft (180 m), and the northern exposure provides remarkably good snow conditions.

WHITEWATER

Box 60

Nelson, B.C.

V1L 5P7

Tel (604) 354-4944

Located about 15 minutes outside of the B.C. city of Nelson, Whitewater is an unbelievable powder skiing mecca that has been dubbed the "Alta of the North." That flattering reference aside, it remains unknown outside of B.C., a fact the local skiers relish. Fortunately, there's plenty of powder to go around, as well as 3,000 acres (1200 ha) of terrain; 2300 ft (700 m) of vertical and up to 320 in (800 cm) of snow annually.

MOUNT WASHINGTON RESORT

Box 3069

Courtenay, B.C.

V9N 5N3

Tel (604) 338-1386

If magenta sunsets, soaring eagles, stunning coastal vistas and 400 in (1000 cm) of snow appeal to you, then Vancouver Island's Mount Washington is a great choice. It's West Coast skiing, Island style. Although its location in the Comox valley near the city of Courtenay is a little out of the way, it's worth the effort it takes to get there. There are over 500 acres (200 ha) of terrain, 1,500 ft (460 m) of vertical, and some of the deepest snow in the Coast Mountains. Slopeside accommodation can be found in a condo village, or try the many motels and hotels in nearby Courtenay.

TOD MOUNTAIN

Box 869

Kamloops, B.C.

V2C 5M8

Tel (604) 578-7222

Located 33 mi (53 km) northeast of Kamloops, Tod Mountain is a towering peak of untapped potential that many experts suggest could be the best ski resort in the B.C. Interior. It has it all, including a vertical drop of 3,100 ft (945 m), 47 runs, numerous bowls, chutes and off-piste options, and over 400 acres (160 ha) of skiable terrain. It also has more than 300 in (760 cm) of light, dry snow annually, and a reputation for some of the toughest skiing in the west. What it doesn't have is on-slope accommodation and a development company with a grand plan and deep pockets. Still, it remains a first-rate skier's mountain that in time could become one of the best in the west.

BLUE MOUNTAIN RESORT

R.R. 3

Collingwood, Ontario

L9Y 3Z2

Tel (705) 445-0231

Ontario is not renowned for its soaring peaks or prodigious natural snowfalls, but it is well known for its large number of superbly run resorts and state-of-the-art computerized snowmaking. Blue Mountain, on the shores of Georgian Bay, is the largest of Ontario's ski areas, and one of the best. It has 29 runs, 700 ft (215 m) of vertical, and top to bottom snowmaking that covers the slopes from November to March with a reliability that's hard to match. Numerous on-slope accommodation options are available, plus plenty more in nearby Collingwood.

HORSESHOE RESORT

Box 10

Horseshoe Valley

R.R. 1

Barrie, Ontario

L4M 4Y8

Tel (705) 835-2790

One of the best resorts for a combination of alpine and cross-country skiing, Horseshoe Valley is also one of the closest "big" resorts to Toronto. In addition to one of the best resort hotels in Ontario, it has a total of 22 alpine slopes and 30 mi (50 km) of nordic trails. The vertical, at a little over 300 ft (90 m), is not the biggest, but it is well served by one quad, two triple and three double chairs, plus top to bottom snowmaking.

MOUNT ST. LOUIS–MOONSTONE

R.R. 4

Coldwater, Ontario

L0K 1E0

Tel (705) 835-2018

This is one of my favorite Ontario resorts, and not just because it's one of the last family-run resorts left in Canada. Mind you, that does help, because the Huter family—led by patriarch Josl—has shown an uncanny ability to meet the demands of a highly competitive market. They were among the first to install quad chairs; they use the summer months to move earth to the top of the mountain to gain vertical; and they run the whole place with a friendliness and efficiency that is noticeable in every aspect from the food in the cafeteria to the grooming of the 44 trails.

OWL'S HEAD

40 chemin Mont Owl's Head

Mansonville, Quebec

J0E 1X0

Tel (514) 292-3342

Owl's Head, in Quebec's Eastern Townships, is often overshadowed by its bigger neighbors, Mont Sutton and Mont Orford, but it's a resort that should be sampled when you're in the region. It has the third highest vertical drop in the province at 1,772 ft (540 m), and the view from the top down the length of Lake Memphrémagog is spectacular. It also has 27 beautifully laid out runs, on-slope accommodation and snowmaking over 80 percent of the mountain.

LE CHANTECLER

1474 chemin Chantecler

Ste-Adèle, Quebec

J0R 1L0

Tel (514) 229-3335

There are few resorts in eastern Canada that are as well suited for families as Chantecler, a tiny perfect resort tucked into a valley just north of the picturesque Laurentian town of Ste-Adèle. At the center of the resort is a European-style hotel, with an indoor pool and sports complex, and ski to your door convenience. Skiing is on four mountain faces, with a total of 22 runs—13 of which are lighted for night skiing—and eight lifts. It's stylish, convenient and just an hour's drive from Montreal.